PRAISE FOR *REUNION*

"If you're suspicious of organized religion, jaded by formulaic flavors of Christianity, or just burnt out trying to do the Religion Thing, *Reunion* is the book for you. A wonderfully warm, engaging, and generous introduction to the personality who stands at the heart of the Christian faith, *Reunion* is a beautiful clarion call for the cynical and world-weary to take a fresh look at Jesus. Whether you're a seeker in search of truth or a disciple in need of a reminder of the wonder and the joy of the gospel, *Reunion* is a beautiful invitation to fall in love—for the first time, or once again—with the Jesus of the New Testament."

—ANDY BANNISTER, SPEAKER FOR RAVI ZACHARIAS INTERNATIONAL MINISTRIES

"I honestly don't know anyone who does a better job of communicating the good news of Jesus in contemporary North American culture than Bruxy Cavey does. Bruxy is witty, winsome, and infectiously passionate about Jesus. All of this shines through in *Reunion*. With a deep understanding of Scripture and a disarming congeniality, *Reunion* lives up to its promise to deliver good news for seekers, saints, and sinners."

—BRIAN ZAHND, AUTHOR OF *FAREWELL TO MARS*

"There is no one better at separating Jesus from the religiosity that has developed around him than Bruxy Cavey. For those of us in churches and for those outside looking in, Jesus too often gets buried or disfigured by religious rules, imported notions of God, and truncated versions of Jesus' message. This book strips those things away and guides the reader to a liberating encounter with Jesus."

—MARK D. BAKER, AUTHOR OF *RELIGIOUS NO MORE*

"Warning: This book contains deep spiritual truths that may radically transform your life. If you read one book about Jesus this year, let this be the one. You'll discover an unexpected freedom and intimately connect with Jesus as never before."

—ANDREW FARLEY, BESTSELLING AUTHOR OF *THE NAKED GOSPEL*

"Bruxy Cavey is one of my favorite communicators and teachers. Bruxy has crafted a beautiful narrative in his presentation of the gospel in his new book. I love the simplicity of the gospel in one word, three words, and thirty words. Bruxy has given us a powerful tool with which to understand the gospel and to share the gospel."

—LESLIE JORDAN, SONGWRITER AND ONE-HALF OF THE WORSHIP DUO ALL SONS & DAUGHTERS

"Within the pages of *Reunion*, you will find good news. Good news that you are not alone. Good news that your questions do not scare God. Good news about religion, the Bible, and staying true to your journey as you seek Jesus. Through his unique blend of pastoral care, self-awareness, and humor, Bruxy Cavey holds our hands and walks with us through the Bible, pointing out the beauty of Jesus all along the way. It's impossible to read this book and not be set free to love Jesus with our whole hearts and seek his kingdom here on earth as it is in heaven."

—OSHETA MOORE, AUTHOR OF *SHALOM SISTAS* AND HOST OF THE SHALOM IN THE CITY PODCAST

"Your quest for God is the most breathtakingly beautiful, challenging journey you can make. If you want to experience a life-changing connection with your Maker, Bruxy Cavey is the ideal guide. *Reunion* is filled with wisdom, humor, and penetrating insights, clearing the path for you to experience the wonder of the Great Mystery."

—KEN SHIGEMATSU, AUTHOR OF *GOD IN MY EVERYTHING* AND SENIOR PASTOR OF TENTH CHURCH

"I don't believe I've ever seen the message of Jesus presented in as clear, as balanced, and as humorous a way as Bruxy has managed to do in *Reunion*. This stimulating and fun book is packed with biblical truths and spiritual insights that will profoundly impact seekers and believers alike. If you or someone you know is wondering what the gospel is all about, or if the version of the gospel you were given just doesn't make sense or doesn't seem like really good news, believe me, this is the book you're looking for!"

—GREGORY A. BOYD, AUTHOR AND SENIOR PASTOR OF WOODLAND HILLS CHURCH

"This book is classic Bruxy: iconoclastic, irreligious, intriguing, and super insightful. Its real gift is that it short-circuits stultifying religion and reintroduces us to the real Jesus. Get ready to have your paradigm rocked. We love this book!"

—DEBRA AND ALAN HIRSCH, AWARD-WINNING AUTHORS AND LEADERS IN THE MISSIONAL CHURCH

"With the skill of an experienced matchmaker, Bruxy Cavey introduces a Jesus worth falling in love with. His vision of relationship beyond religion is personal enough to change a life and powerful enough to change the world."

—MEGHAN GOOD, TEACHING PASTOR AT TRINITY MENNONITE CHURCH

"This book is like Bruxy: disarming, big-hearted, down-to-earth, and dripping with Jesus, without the stench of religious hypocrisy. And it's funny! Imagine if the Dude from The Big Lebowski loved in such ways that made you laugh-open-your-heart to reimagine Christian faith to look more like Christ. That's Bruxy. And his big-bear-hugging heart is on each page for the seekers, the saints, and us sinners alike."

—JARROD MCKENNA, TEACHING PASTOR AT WESTCITY CHURCH IN AUSTRALIA AND COFOUNDER OF THE FIRST HOME PROJECT

"Bruxy is a weird pastor who leads an unusual church, but that probably makes him qualified to write a book that makes sense to regular people with all their quirks. I've benefited so much from listening to his teaching, and this book brings together a funny yet profound encapsulation of what the gospel is and how it changes everything."

—JUSTIN BRIERLEY, HOST OF THE *UNBELIEVABLE?* RADIO SHOW AND PODCAST

"A lively, compelling invitation to meet the real Jesus. Delightfully humorous and solidly biblical, Cavey powerfully presents both the challenge and joy of embracing Christ. *Reunion* is both a winsome introduction to Jesus for seekers and an enriching refresher for longtime disciples. Simply excellent."

—RON SIDER, PRESIDENT EMERITUS OF EVANGELICALS FOR SOCIAL ACTION

PRAISE FOR BRUXY CAVEY

"A fresh voice calling people out of the twenty-first-century wilderness."

—JIM WALLIS, PRESIDENT OF SOJOURNERS AND CALL TO RENEWAL

"Finally, someone who does a brilliant job at pulling back the curtain of the spoon-fed, cookie-cutter, navel-gazing nonsense we see within Christendom as well as ourselves."

—DREW MARSHALL, HOST OF *THE DREW MARSHALL SHOW*

"A voice that deserves the widest possible exposure."

—BRIAN MCLAREN, AUTHOR OF *THE GREAT SPIRITUAL MIGRATION*

(re)union

(re)union

the GOOD NEWS
of JESUS
for SEEKERS, SAINTS,
and SINNERS

BRUXY CAVEY
foreword by SHANE CLAIBORNE

Herald Press
Harrisonburg, Virginia

Herald Press
PO Box 866, Harrisonburg, Virginia 22803
www.HeraldPress.com

Library and Archives Canada Cataloguing in Publication
Cavey, Bruxy, 1965-, author
      Reunion : the good news of Jesus for seekers, saints, and sinners / Bruxy
Cavey.
Issued in print and electronic formats.
ISBN 978-1-5138-0139-1 (hardcover).--ISBN 978-1-5138-0133-9 (ebook)
      1. Jesus Christ--Teachings. I. Title.
BS2415.C38 2017   232.9'54   C2016-907122-7
                                                                  C2016-907123-5

All Scripture quotations, unless otherwise indicated, are taken from the *Holy Bible,
New International Version®, NIV®*. Copyright ©1973, 1978, 1984, 2011 by Biblica,
Inc.™ Used by permission of Zondervan. All rights reserved worldwide. www.zonder-
van.com The "NIV" and "New International Version" are trademarks registered in the
United States Patent and Trademark Office by Biblica, Inc.™

REUNION
© 2017 by Bruxy Cavey
Released by Herald Press, Harrisonburg, Virginia 22803. 800-245-7894.
All rights reserved.
Library of Congress Control Number: 2016957672
Canadian Entry Numbers: C2016-907122-7; C2016-907123-5
International Standard Book Number: 978-1-5138-0130-8
International Standard Book Number (hardcover): 978-1-5138-0139-1
International Standard Book Number (ebook): 978-1-5138-0133-9
Printed in the United States of America
Cover and interior design by Reuben Graham

22 21 20 19 18   13 12 11 10 9 8 7 6 5 4

To Nina,
who shows me Jesus
every day.

CONTENTS

FOREWORD

I love Bruxy Cavey. He has a pastor's heart and a prophet's fire. *Reunion* is a book about Jesus. And it is a good book about Jesus. Jesus drips from every page, every word, every story in this book. Because Jesus oozes from Bruxy Cavey. Bruxy wants a Christianity that looks like Jesus again. He wants Christians to be known for love again. He wants us all to fall in love with Jesus and to allow Jesus to reorient everything. Now the last are first, the first are last. The mighty are cast from their thrones, and the lowly are lifted up. The hungry are filled with good things, and the rich are sent away empty. The poor are blessed, and the peacemakers are the children of God. That's the upside-down kingdom that Jesus talked about and that you will find in this book.

Ironically, and sadly, one of the biggest obstacles to Christ has sometimes been Christians. We often look very unlike the Christ we worship. Too often we've become known more for whom we've excluded than whom we've embraced, more for what we are against than what we are for. Sometimes we've become known for the very things Jesus spoke out *against*. We aren't always known for the key virtue by which Jesus said people will recognize those of us who belong to him: *love*. As Reverend William Barber has said, "When we stop focusing on Jesus, we end up talking a lot about things Jesus didn't talk much about and we don't talk about the things Jesus had a whole lot to say about."

When it comes to religion in North America, the fastest-growing groups are the "nones" (the unaffiliated), the ex-Catholics, and the recovering evangelicals. One of the reasons these groups are growing so quickly is because they see the contradictions of Christians so clearly.

Many folks outside the faith have come to see Christians, and evangelicals in particular, as anti-women, anti-gay, anti-environment, and anti-immigrant, and as the champions of guns and war. The things that have come to characterize evangelicalism often directly contradict the core values and teachings of Christ.

A new generation loves Jesus and cares about justice. Many of them love Jesus but are embarrassed by Christians. The things that have come to characterize Christianity seem to be at odds with Christ. They care about life: the earth, the poor, refugees, and immigrants. They know that black lives matter and that racism is real. For them, a consistent ethic of life shapes the way they think about war and militarism, gun violence and police brutality, the death penalty and mass incarceration. To be pro-life does not just mean to be anti-abortion; it is about being *for life*. And it is an inconsistent ethic of life that has caused many of these post-evangelicals to jump ship from the church.

And that is where Bruxy Cavey is a gift—to the church and to the world. In this book, Bruxy will share with you the gospel, the "good news," which he puts in one word: *Jesus*.

As Bruxy will show you so well, Jesus is the lens through which we understand the Bible and the world. When we want to know what God is like, we look at Jesus. When we want to know how to live, we look to Jesus. When Scriptures seem to be in conflict with one another, we let Jesus be the referee. As I have heard Bruxy say so beautifully: "We believe in the authoritative, inerrant, infallible Word of God. His name is Jesus."

One of my neighbors was talking to me about how we over-complicate things, especially theological things—like the idea of incarnation. Spanish is her first language, and she explained to me that incarnation is not that complex. When you order your burrito *con carne*, it means "with meat." That's what the incarnation is about: God *con carne*. Jesus is God in the flesh. God with meat. Love with skin on.

Christians are meant to join that incarnation, the manifestation of God's love. We are to be a part of fleshing out God's love in the world. We are to remind the world of Jesus, to give off the fragrance of Christ as we live. We are to live in such a way that we can say with the apostle Paul: "I no longer live, but Christ lives in me" (Galatians 2:20).

This book is about the kind of Christianity that lives as if Jesus meant the stuff he said. And that is what Bruxy Cavey is about. I am honored to call him a friend and a brother.

—*Shane Claiborne, activist, speaker,
and bestselling author of* Irresistible
Revolution *and* Executing Grace

PREFACE
GO FLY A KITE

There is something in each human being that
reaches out for God, and that reaching instance
comes from God and leads to God.
—SCOT MCKNIGHT

My first experience of flying a kite was a flurry of fun and failure. My father helped me get it flying, and it seemed as if I had everything under control. But when he was distracted for a moment, my kite crashed. I claimed that the wind pulled the string out of my hand. But to be honest, I let it go on purpose.

As a boy I had a vivid imagination, and I often personified my toys. To me, my new kite was a person, deserving of the freedom to explore its own potential. It seemed to pull away on purpose, struggling to be completely free of the constraints of the string and my guiding grip. (Ya, I was a weird kid.) I felt I was holding it back from flying as high as it could fly and going wherever it wanted to go. So I let go.

At first there was a flutter of freedom and flight. But it was short-lived, and the maiden voyage of Bruxy's first kite ended with a nosedive into dirt.

The untethered kite is a vivid picture of what can happen to the human soul. Whether consciously or not, humans aspire to something more than this mundane earthbound existence. Like migratory birds or butterflies with a mysterious homing instinct, we are compelled to travel. We have a nagging sense that we are made for Something More.

According to Jesus, we are always being drawn heavenward by the wind of the Spirit, the breath of God. Our problem is that once we are enthralled with our potential, many of us make a fatal mistake: we assume that complete autonomy is our birthright, and we detach ourselves from anything we perceive as limiting us. This is the story of humanity.

Some of us turn to a kind of generic spirituality or self-identify as "a person of faith." But generic spirituality never satisfies our souls, any more than the *concept* of marriage soothes our loneliness. Faith, like love, is always about the *person* in whom we have faith.

This book is for people who sense they are free-floating kites in need of reconnection to a guiding hand. Perhaps life is fairly good for you these days, but you sense the possibility of an impending nosedive. Perhaps you've already hit the ground, and life has fallen apart. Or perhaps you are simply curious—a spiritual seeker who wants to know more about Jesus.

Consider this: like kites, we weren't made for complete detachment. We need (re)union with God. This is a book about the good news of Jesus, the one who keeps our spirituality connected to the Truth and enables us to soar.

—*Bruxy*

PART I

1

THE GOOD NEWS
IN A TATTOO

*Christianity is no ordinary religion: it is at the very least, and
since the beginning, the religion of the end of religion.*

—GIL ANIDJAR

LEVITICUS 19:28. These large black letters and numbers are inked
into my left forearm. It's the only tattoo I've been inspired to
get. (Besides a completely failed attempt to have my wedding ring
tattooed on my finger—it faded away within months. Bad omen?
Let's move on.)

I wanted a Bible verse that summed up the good news message
of Jesus in a tattoo, and Leviticus 19:28 seemed like the obvious choice.

So what does Leviticus 19:28 say? Thanks for asking. That's
the Bible verse that says, "Thou shalt not get a tattoo."

I know. Now I have some explaining to do.

SHAVE AND A HAIRCUT

When I was a kid, I had a Sunday school teacher who was, well,
less than joyful: Mrs. Grumpy Pants, as we liked to call her. I
remember the time a man with tattoos on his arm came to church.
"I hope he gets saved," I heard Mrs. G. mutter, and I wondered

what she meant by that. "You can tell this man doesn't love God
because he has a bunch of tattoos," Mrs. G. explained to me, "and
the Bible clearly says it's an abomination to get a tattoo." (*Abomination* always sounds like a serious sin upgrade from just a regular
trespass or transgression.)

This was very disappointing news, since I wanted to get a tattoo
when I grew up. I asked Mrs. G., "What if I got a tattoo of Jesus?
Or maybe a Bible verse?" Her look of disapproval did not soften.

Later in life I learned that the one Bible verse that discour-
ages tattoos appears in Leviticus 19. This is the same chapter that
teaches other important things: Men must never cut their hair or
trim their beards. (Three cheers for hippies!) Farmers must never
plant two kinds of crops in the same fields or harvest their fields
right to the edges. (Not a farmer? Me neither. So we're good here.)
And everyone must avoid wearing clothing that is woven with
two different kinds of material. (Pure wool? Check. Pure cotton?
Check. Polyester blend? We'll stone you.)

Obviously, Christians don't feel the need to obey every verse
of the Bible. But this chapter also includes rich teaching such as
respect your parents, don't curse people who are deaf or put stum-
bling blocks in front of people who are blind (how practical), and
even one of Jesus' favorites—love your neighbor as yourself. So
how do we get to pick and choose what to follow and what to
forget, what to obey and what to ignore?

The urgency for Bible-believing people to figure out how to
actually apply the teaching from their own Bibles only increases
the more you read. Should we go to war against nations who don't
embrace our God? Should we burn witches and stone to death our
rebellious children? And what about the list of personal defects
that disqualify priests from serving God in Leviticus 21?[1] Bad skin,
bad posture, bad eyesight, a broken bone, or just too short to ride

---

1. Although these restrictions only applied to priests, Pharisees as well as the early
Christ-followers believed in the priesthood of all believers. Which makes these
restrictions especially troublesome.

the ride: it's easy to be disqualified from approaching the altar of God.

Trying to figure out how to be a good Christian while obeying the Bible's rules is exhausting, even soul crushing. I can understand why the writings of the New Testament contrast the old way of the letter of the law with the new way of the Spirit by saying, "The letter kills, but the Spirit gives life" (2 Corinthians 3:6).

THE END OF THE OLD

If you open any Christian Bible, you'll notice it is divided into two sections: the Old Testament and the New Testament. *Testament* is another word for *covenant*, which in this case refers to a way of living in relationship with God. So the Bible is divided into the old way of living and the new way of living. And although there is continuity, the two ways are radically different.

The old way of living, the Old Testament, is pre-Jesus. It describes God's covenant of promise and trust with humankind (as with Adam and Abraham) that then became a covenant of law-keeping and sacrifice-making (through Moses). Because people grew hardhearted and hurtful toward others and themselves, God intervened with laws to keep them in line, rituals to help them focus on what is important, and sacrifices to help them see the gravity of their sin and turn to God for forgiveness.[2]

Then, when Jesus came, God inaugurated the new covenant—which is to say, he changed everything.

A first-century Christ-follower wrote about the contrast between the old way of religion and the new way of Jesus. "By calling this covenant 'new,' he has made the first one obsolete; and what is obsolete and outdated will soon disappear" (Hebrews 8:13). Obsolete? Outdated? On its way out? Now them's fightin' words. (I'm considering getting HEBREWS 8:13 on my other arm.)

---

2. Usually, when Christians refer to the "old covenant" they are not referring to the covenant of intimacy with Adam, or the covenant of promise with Noah, or the covenant of faith with Abraham, but the Mosaic covenant of laws, rituals, and sacrifices that dominates most of the Old Testament and was in full operation in Jesus' day.

Here we have a verse from the New Testament saying that the Old Testament is over. This is astounding: one part of the Bible calling another part of the Bible "obsolete."

This isn't a contradiction; the old covenant contains prophecies about the coming of a new covenant that would supersede the old (e.g., Jeremiah 31:31-34). This is an intentional change, a planned and purposed development in human spiritual history. If you believe that God is behind all of this, it's a cosmic shift in how our world works.

In English, we can use the word *old* in two different ways: (1) aged, or (2) former. If your friend tells you, "I really like my old boss," she might mean she is enjoying working for her current boss, who happens to be older. But she probably means she misses working for her former boss.

The Greek word for "obsolete" in Hebrews 8:13 is the word for "old," as in something that is former, over, worn out, in the past. It's like an old boyfriend or girlfriend: we've moved on.

At the same time, although Jesus taught that he had come to bring about the end of the way of law and sacrifice, he also claimed that the teaching of the Scriptures would somehow endure (see Matthew 5:17-19 and Luke 16:16-17). So we don't throw out the first half of our Bibles, but we read the Old Testament as "the story of what doesn't work." The Old Testament endures as God's way of reminding us that we don't need more rules and rituals; in fact, rules and rituals can often get in the way of what we really need, which is God himself.

When we pursue the rules instead of the Ruler, the laws instead of Spirit, the sacrifices instead of the One who became the last sacrifice, we're not getting closer to God; we're reaching for an obsolete system that God has long since abandoned. Jesus came to clear the way for a more direct intimacy with the Almighty.

So why did I get LEVITICUS 19:28 tattooed on my arm? As a reminder that Jesus claimed to fulfill the system and make the old obsolete (Matthew 5:17). This clears the way for something better.

It's the good news in a tattoo: Jesus came to save us not only from our sin, but also from our religion.

KNOWING GOD MEANS "NO-ING" RELIGION

This irreligious aspect of the gospel raises all kinds of questions about religion today, including and especially the Christian religion. And we'll get to those later in this book. For now, I want to offer you hope—especially if you have been hurt or disappointed by religion—that Jesus is on your side.

Near the end of his life on earth, Jesus prayed to his heavenly Father.[3] He said these words: "Now this is eternal life: that they know you, the only true God, and Jesus Christ, whom you have sent" (John 17:3).

When someone I trust starts a sentence with "Now this is eternal life," I pay attention to what comes next. For Jesus, what follows is not religion, not tradition, not the Ten Commandments, the 613 Laws, the Eightfold Path, the Four Noble Truths, the Five Pillars of Action, the Six Articles of Belief, the Seven Sacraments, nor any other of the systems of salvation stewarded by the religions of our planet.

Instead, Jesus said eternal life is knowing God, and knowing Jesus. This is religion-free faith.

In Bible days, the verb "to know" meant more than just intellectual knowledge, especially when used the way Jesus does here—about knowing persons. To really know a person meant to have a deep and intimate *union* with that person, which is why to "know" someone was commonly used as a euphemism for sex (for example, Matthew 1:25 KJV reflects the original Greek when it says that Mary was a virgin because Joseph "knew her not till she had brought forth her firstborn son").

This knowing is about more than information; it's about intimacy. *Knowing* someone is far more than knowing *about* someone.

---

3. Wait! How could Jesus *be* God and *talk to* God at the same time? The answer lies in the elemental nature of God as love, which is to say, God as persons-in-relationship. More about this in chapter 3.

We could study someone's online profile and social media presence all day, but that doesn't mean we know that person. Yet at the same time, intimacy is indeed enhanced by an appropriate amount of information.

Jesus came to lead us into an intimate experience with God, a kind of reunion with God through our union with Christ. That's what he meant by saying eternal life was knowing God and knowing Jesus. And this "knowing" will include intimate experience as well as intimacy-enhancing information. That's what this book is all about.

Because Jesus is the focus of the gospel, my hope is that reading this book will help you not only know *about* Jesus, who helps us know *about* God. My prayer is that this book—a book about (re)union—will help you get to *know* God and *know* Jesus, God's full revelation of himself.

Know God.

No religion.

A LESSON FROM OTHELLO

"A minute to learn, a lifetime to master." I love this slogan for the board game Othello. When I play a new game, I want to be able to get in the game as soon as possible, but I also don't want it to be overly simplistic. I want the gameplay to be easy to learn, but I also want it to leave room for my growth as a player.

"A minute to learn, a lifetime to master" could also describe the good news of Jesus. There is a simplicity to the gospel, so that even (and especially) a child can comprehend it. There is also a depth and infinite richness to the gospel, which means that we can all spend the rest of our lives learning, discussing, and applying its truths.

In this book I'm going to take a progressive approach, from simplicity to increased complexity. We will talk about how the gospel can be summed up in one word, three words, and thirty words. These aren't different messages, but different degrees of detail to the same message.

Understanding the gospel in its simplicity and fullness will help us understand our origin, destiny, and identity—who we are, why we matter, and how we can become the best version of ourselves in this world.

I have been studying this message for decades, and I still have regular "Aha!" experiences as I notice some aspect or application of the gospel that hadn't dawned on me before. That is why this book, and any book about the gospel, is necessarily incomplete. This book is a finite summary of an infinitely wonderful message, written by someone who is still mid-journey toward a full grasp of just how good this good news really is. In the words of the apostle Paul, speaking about his desire to one day be with God face-to-face, "Now I know in part; then I shall know fully, even as I am fully known" (1 Corinthians 13:12).[4]

Still, our unavoidably partial and incomplete knowledge of God is no excuse for ignoring any of the obvious and key elements of the message of Jesus. Yet it seems as though this is precisely what has happened for large segments of church history.

For instance, while the Christian church has been consistent in proclaiming the good news of God's love for the world and for-giveness for sin, it has often misrepresented or underrepresented the gospel of God's kingdom on earth, here and now. As we'll see, Jesus' message about the kingdom of God lived out in this life has powerful implications for how we prioritize peace, reconcili-ation, and enemy love in relationship with God and with others. Ignore this aspect of the gospel, and we are left with a religion that proclaims love and forgiveness while it advances through violent attitudes and actions.

Another example of a great gospel omission is the focus of chapter 10: the irreligious implications embedded in the good news of Jesus. Church history records long periods of time when Chris-tians interpreted Christ's confrontation with the Jewish religion of his day as a challenge to the *Jewish* religion, rather than to the

---

4. No doubt, Paul is here referring to the "knowing" of both intimacy and information.

Jewish *religion*. In other words, the church neutralized the inherent rebuke to religion embedded in Jesus' message by interpreting it as a rebuke of Judaism alone. But the message and mission of Jesus is a universal rebuke to all religion, of his day and every day, including and especially the Christian religion. Of course, how could the Christian church proclaim the inherently irreligious nature of the message of Jesus when they were stewarding one of the largest and most powerful religions on the planet? It's a pickle.

It seems that the message of Jesus changed the world . . . until the world changed the message. We domesticated and emasculated the full and forceful gospel of Jesus, settling instead for a fragmented and facile version. But I'm happy to say that there is a growing movement of truth-seekers and Jesus-lovers who are calling for a return to the first and foundational good news message of Jesus. This book is inspired by them, and it is an invitation to join their ranks.

SHOULD YOU BE READING THIS?

Sometimes publishers talk about the "target audience" for a book. Who does the author have in mind when writing? For me, the target is pretty big. If you're human, the gospel is for you.

But if I had to narrow it down, as the subtitle suggests, I'm writing to three kinds of readers. Primarily, this book is for spiritual *seekers*: people who are open to God, spiritually curious, and interested in Jesus. (If you see yourself more as a skeptic than a seeker, put off by the hypocrisy and judgmentalism of religion, I recommend you read my previous book, *The End of Religion*.)

Secondarily, I'm writing to Christian *saints* who want to dig deeper into their own faith. Sometimes religion, including and especially the Christian religion, can be one of our biggest barriers to seeing Jesus clearly. I'm hoping this book will renew your joy in the gospel and help you learn how to better live and share this good news with others. Some Christians treat the good news of Jesus as simply a salvation message—an invitation to be saved by grace through faith—and then expect to move on from the gospel to something else, something deeper. But we should never see the gospel in our rearview mirror. We do not measure our spiritual growth by the distance we put between us and the gospel. The gospel is our GPS for life.

Lastly, this book is for *sinners*—those of us who are aware of our brokenness, our failure, and the distance we've put between God and ourselves. For you, *Reunion* is an invitation to fully accept God's forgiveness and experience his embrace.

Whether this is just the beginning of a lifelong journey for you or a midpoint pause to refuel along the way, I'm very excited for what lies ahead. It will be an incredible journey of discovery.

WHERE WE ARE HEADED

We can never reduce the good news to a single sound bite. Jesus used different means to communicate the gospel's rich truths, including direct explanation, symbolic stories, and provocative actions. Likewise, the earliest Jesus-followers communicated the gospel in a variety of ways, without repeating any one phrase as the totality of God's good news for us.

Over the years, Christians have tried to summarize the gospel as a series of steps to peace with God or as a set of spiritual laws. These can be helpful—as long as we always remember that these summaries are pointers to the gospel and not the fullness of the gospel itself. Though simple, the gospel is multidimensional.

So, is "God loves you and has a wonderful plan for your life" the gospel? Yes. Is it the fullness of the gospel? No way. Is "Jesus died on the cross for our sins and rose again so we can be reconciled with God" the gospel? Absolutely. Is it the fullness of the gospel? Not even close.

The same is true for the different approaches to summarizing the gospel that I take in this book. No one summary is enough, but each of our one-, three-, and thirty-word approaches will be helpful for thinking clearly about some aspect of the gospel.

Think of the one-, three-, and thirty-word approaches as concentric circles, with the one-word gospel as the bull'seye surrounded by the three-word gospel, then fully fleshed out by the thirty-word gospel. Our expanded study of the gospel in thirty words will allow us to examine in more detail different aspects of the gospel, such as the foundation, or ground, of the gospel, the four gifts that God offers us through the gospel, and the ultimate goal of the gospel.

The fullness of God's good news to us is infinite in its scope and eternal in its implications. We'll spend the rest of eternity plumbing the depths of this message. Still, it is my hope that this book will offer you enough of the gospel to allow you to

- think clearly about the gospel;
- respond unreservedly to the gospel; and
- invite others to consider the gospel.

HOW TO READ THIS BOOK

Hopefully you are reading this book for transformation and not just information. If so, I'd like to recommend reading it in three ways.

First, read *reflectively*. Take your time and read *beneath* the lines. I'm convinced that the subject matter we're dealing with here is worthy of contemplation as you go and of application when you pause. Look up the Bible passages listed and see for yourself if what I'm saying is accurate. You may also want to mark up the text as you go, take notes in the margins, make use of a notebook, and check out the additional online study materials.

Second, read *prayerfully*. You may or may not be at a place in your life where prayer comes naturally, or you may not even be convinced that there is a God to pray to. If so, for you, prayer may feel as if talking to someone who may not exist, and that seems weird. Yet, when you enter a house and you wonder if there is anybody home, one of the best ways to find out is to call out, "Hello? Is there anybody here?" Maybe there is no one home, and you were just talking to yourself when you called out, but it was a reasonable risk to take and one that helps you discover the truth. On the other hand, maybe there *is* someone home, and maybe that someone will answer back. I pray that you'll hear God through your intuition, your imagination, your conscience, and through others who are with you along your journey. Most of all, I'm praying that you'll hear God speaking through the words and actions of Jesus.

Third, read it *relationally*. If possible, turn this book into a conversation. Share it with a friend and talk about what you're learning. Perhaps someone gave you this book. If so, start there: talk together about it all. Or start a book study with a few friends. This book is meant to lead to conversation, not just contemplation. The gospel is a relational message, and it will be best absorbed in a relational context.

And if you end up reading this book alone, remember you are not really alone. Others are reading and praying and discussing and applying what you are learning in these pages. Reading a book can sometimes seem solitary. But as you move closer to the person and proclamation of Jesus, you are becoming part of something bigger: a Jesus movement that stretches around the world and back through time. And if the God that Jesus talked about is real, he has already been active in your life long before you first picked up this book. Whether or not you have sensed it, it's quite possible that God got you to this place right here, right now, holding this book and reading these words. And God will continue to work in your life as you move forward along the way.

LANGUAGE LIMITS

Before we move on, let's address one more important note here: I sometimes refer to God in male terms to best align my language with the Bible and because of the firm conviction that God is personal love, not impersonal energy. We have no neuter personal pronouns in English, just like the biblical languages of Hebrew and Greek, and I cannot refer to Ultimate Reality as an "it" without doing damage to the worldview of Jesus. We know that God is beyond gender and that maleness and femaleness equally reflect his image and likeness in different, complementary, and beautiful ways. So, while I understand why the biblical writers referred to God as "him" and I will join them in this practice, we should keep in mind that we are talking about a God who transcends and yet manifests the best of both genders.

I lament the limits of language when talking about God. But I suppose that comes with the territory. We should expect our human-made mechanism for communication to be stretched to the limits when talking about the infinite, incomprehensible, and eternal Energy we call God.

Thankfully, the good news is that once upon a time, God went beyond words and sent his Word to us in human form.

2

HOW TO HOLD DYNAMITE

*You Christians look after a document containing enough
dynamite to blow all civilization to pieces, turn the world
upside down, and bring peace to a battle-torn planet. But you
treat it as though it is nothing more than a piece of literature.*

— MOHANDAS GANDHI

I stood there, frozen. I couldn't speak or move or even think. Paralysis had overtaken my body, and I felt as if I had entered into some sort of existential stasis in which time stopped. Hundreds of people stared at me, waiting for some sort of response.

I had just heard these words: "Bruxy Cavey, will you marry me?"

Nina and I had been dating for years, and we had been good friends for years before that. I knew I wanted to marry her, but I had been hurt in previous relationships and I was still carrying around those past pains. Having been rejected before, I had started to view myself as undesirable, so I worried that Nina's professed love for me was really just an act of pity. She must want to rescue me, I thought. So here we were, letting the time pass, almost married but never committing. Thankfully, Nina was secure enough, and knew my heart well enough, to make the move.

At the church I serve as senior pastor, The Meeting House, we end most Sunday services with a question and answer time. We call it Q & Eh? (after all, we're Canadians). And on that Sunday, my girlfriend, Nina, came to church with a Q. Turns out it was the Q of all Qs.

Nina was the first to raise her hand when I asked, "Who has a question?" When someone handed her the microphone, rather than ask her question sitting in her seat or standing in front of it, she stepped up *onto* her seat, as if she was about to make some sort of announcement. I remember thinking, Hmm. This is unusual. Maybe this is Pastor Appreciation Day and Nina is about to make a speech?

Right after she popped the question—"Bruxy Cavey, will you marry me?"—friends who were planted in the congregation stood up and waved giant signs. The signs read:

SAY YES!

MAKE AN HONEST WOMAN OF HER!

JUST DO IT!

IT'S ABOUT TIME!

IF YOU DON'T I WILL! (I never liked that guy.)

JOHN 3:16! (Just because.)

I didn't know it then, but hundreds of balloons were well hidden and all set to be dropped from the ceiling. (Nina had the foresight to ask the balloon people not to drop them until I said yes. She could envision the morbidly surreal scene in which I would say "I'm sorry, I can't"—the room would be filled with gasps, followed by deathly shocked silence; Nina would break into tears; and balloons would fall in the eerie stillness, like giant clown teardrops.)

So there I was, frozen, with the entire church staring at me waiting for my reaction. Then, after what felt like a year or two, I began to feel something. Warmth. Peace. Value. It was pouring over me. I felt wanted. I felt loved. I felt worth the risk. I ran off the platform down to where Nina was and we hugged for a long time, surrounded by a cheering, applauding crowd. By this point I was crying too much to talk. I whispered yes in her ear, and Nina yelled out to everyone else, "He said yes!" (Cue the balloons.)

That Nina wanted to marry me was the best news I could have received at that moment. It was absolutely powerful in a way I'd never experienced power. Now, many years later, I can say that moment changed my life. It exploded my lousy concept of myself and my fears about the future.

It was like dynamite.

BEST NEWS EVER

Take a moment right now and try to imagine the best news you could ever receive. Visualize the moment, the person giving you the news, and how you react. What, for you, would be the best news possible? Is it about money? Overcoming illness? A reconciled relationship? Does it revolve around possessions, power, or love? How would it change your life for the better? How does it make you *feel* to picture that coming true?

Whatever your imagination could dream up is still not as good as the good news you're about to receive through this book. I know that is a bold statement, and it might make you feel skeptical. But on this topic, I am absolutely confident.

An early follower of Jesus once said that he was not ashamed of this good news because the message itself is "the power of God" at work in the hearts of people who really hear it, receive it, and believe it (Romans 1:16). The word *power* in that verse is a translation of the Greek word *dunamis*, from which we get our English word *dynamite*. This good news—the core message about the core mission of Jesus—is God's explosive energy. There is something about this message of Jesus that is inherently powerful.

But while dynamite explodes and destroys, the power of this good news heals, restores, and reconciles. It can change minds, save lives, and renew relationships. Truth does this. Ultimate truth does this ultimately. Mind you, it can also explode, demolish, and destroy any lies that we have allowed to erode our intimacy with God and our understanding of ourselves.

WHAT'S IN A WORD?

The message Jesus brought has the power to change our lives, inside out and upside down. This message is so transformative, for individuals and their relationships, that it has its own name. Jesus and his earliest followers called it the "gospel," which means "good news." But it means more than just good news as opposed to bad news. The early Christians used it to mean *the* good news. It is the best possible news; the best news you will ever get. This is the news you've been waiting to hear, hoping to find, and longing to know. That's gospel.

The word *gospel* comes from the Old English word *godspell*, meaning "good tale" or "good story." Translators chose it to represent what in the original texts of the Bible is a Greek word: *euangelion*. In Latin, it's *evangelium*.

This is where we get several contemporary English words. *Evangel*: the good news of Jesus. *Evangelism* and *evangelize*: the act of spreading, or to spread, the good news. *Evangelistic*: describing people who actively share their faith. *Evangelist*: one who does evangelism, sometimes combined with a prefix for *television* to produce *televangelist*, meaning one who smells of cheese.

And it's where we get the often misunderstood word *evangelical*. In some countries, the word *evangelical* has become synonymous with religious and political conservatives, whereas it simply means "people who are all about the good news of Jesus." This is why when people ask me, "So Bruxy, are you one of those *evangelical* Christians?" I have to first ask them what they mean. Do they mean a person who delights in the simple life-changing message of Jesus, who wants to become more like him, and who enjoys sharing this good news with others? I hope so. Do they mean a person who is part of a religious subculture known for its judgmental attitudes, political conservatism, and preachy bumper stickers? I hope not.

BIRTH ANNOUNCEMENT

Of course, if the gospel of Jesus really is good news for everyone, this also has implications for how private we should be about this message. Most people practice tolerance for other people's faith as long as they keep it to themselves. But if I have good news for you and I keep it to myself, this is not kindness but unkindness. We are talking about news that is wonderful and that is for everyone. The gospel is an announcement that is meant to be shared.

When an ancient empire won a war against an aggressive enemy so that times of safety, peace, and prosperity would be ushered in, the message of this victory was announced far and wide as *euangelion*—gospel. When new royalty was born, the announcement carried throughout the land was called *euangelion*—gospel. When something wonderfully "world changing" happened, heralds carried the message to all points of the known world, calling it *euangelion*—gospel.

We see this demonstrated clearly in history when, for instance, the Roman proconsul Paulus Fabius Maximus honored Caesar Augustus by referring to the day of his birth as "*euangelion* [gospel] for the whole world."

Jesus and his earliest followers chose this word—*euangelion*—to summarize his good news message of hope and healing, of reconciled relationships and (re)union with God. This is more than just a *spiritual* message, a *devotional* message, or a message of *faith*. The gospel is all of those things, but it is also so much more. The good news of Jesus points to a very *this-worldly* (as opposed to otherworldly) spirituality, with implications for how we live in relation to politics, commerce, and certainly our day-to-day relationships. So the gospel is good news intended to be shared far and wide. The gospel is an announcement for all people about a world-changing event, an offer of peace and reconciliation from God to absolutely everyone.

When Jesus was born, an angel announced his birth to shepherds in the fields as "good news that will cause great joy for all the people" (Luke 2:10).

Good news.

Great joy.

All people.

That is gospel.

WHEN GOOD NEWS GOES BAD

If the gospel really is good news of great joy, it is a purely positive message. This has implications for how the gospel is thought about, discussed, and shared with others. Any conversation about the gospel should be accompanied by a positive emotional atmosphere, one filled with joy and hope for everyone. Too often, religious people have preached the content of the gospel while yelling in angry tones, as though angry yelling was important for displaying spiritual passion. (It is not.)

When proclaimed that way, angry gospel preaching (an oxymoronic concept, to be sure) creates an inherent dissonance between the substance of the message and the spirit in which it is given. What should be heard as a *good* news message is preached as though it were *bad* news. This creates more heat than light, as much confusion as it does conviction.

So if you've been hurt or insulted or offended in the name of Jesus by someone who has confused zeal with anger and truth with criticism, then I want to apologize here and now. If you've been burned by conservative Christianity and its yelly preachers, I am sorry. Jesus taught us to leave the judging up to God. It is an ironic tragedy that any who call themselves Christians should be judgmental, bigoted, or anything other than loving, gracious, joyful, and kind.

It's true that some good news only makes sense in light of bad news, especially if the good news is a solution to a problem. If your doctor said, "I have good news for you: I think you have a good chance to beat this cancer," that would only feel like good news if you were already aware that you had cancer. Otherwise this "good news" would sound like the worst news you've heard in a long time. Somewhere along the line we will need to do some honest assessing of the problem to which the gospel is the solution (we will get to the problem later in the book). And there may be aspects of the message and mission of Jesus that might sound like bad news to some people because they are offensive to certain people—especially religiously conservative people. But that should never be an excuse to offend others through one's tone, attitude, or judgmental disposition.

For now, let's not miss what should be clear: the gospel is joyful news, happy-making news, news worth celebrating. This joy should always be our disposition when we listen to, learn about, and pass on the good news of Jesus.

OUR DEEPEST NEED

The gospel is a message about union with God—a reunion, of sorts, with the One who gives our lives meaning and purpose. And in the process of our understanding and embrace of this message, the gospel will also address a constellation of other basic human needs.

Acceptance.

Forgiveness.

Purpose.

Security.

Over the years, I've seen this good news affect many lives in many ways, especially these four areas. The good news of Jesus meets our fundamental human needs for acceptance through God's love, forgiveness through God's grace, purpose through the mission of the kingdom, and security in God's rest from religion.

Abraham Maslow, arguably one of the most influential psychologists of the last century, is famous for crafting his "hierarchy of needs." As it is presented in most psychology textbooks, this pyramid of priorities ranks human needs by starting at the ground level with physical and safety needs, moving up the pyramid through relational and psychological needs, and ending at the pinnacle with "self-actualization."

What most people don't realize is that this presentation reflects Maslow's earlier thinking, which he later modified to add one more level of ultimate need above self-actualization: *self-transcendence*. The highest of all human needs is the need to move beyond ourselves, to be freed from our own ego addiction. Our highest need is to know and be known by something greater than ourselves, and to participate in that higher reality. In the words of Augustine of Hippo, "You have made us for yourself, O Lord, and our hearts are restless until they rest in you."

BEFORE THE BEGINNING

When my daughter Maya was eight years old, we decided it was time to watch the entire Star Wars saga as a family, starting at the very beginning: *Episode IV—A New Hope*. We had done a fairly successful job of keeping spoilers away from Maya so she could have some of the same surprise moments many of us did when we were kids—Obi Wan's sacrifice, Darth Vader's paternal revelation, Luke and Leia's sibling relationship, and even Vader's eventual redemption.

When the rolling credits began, I noticed Maya looked puzzled, but we kept going. Eventually, a few minutes into the movie, Maya asked if we could pause to talk. Her questions ran something like this: *Episode IV? A New Hope?* What was the *old* hope? Why did they need *any* hope? And what happened to episodes 1, 2, and 3? (I told her they didn't exist, and we're keeping that secret.) Why is that golden robot British? Why is that tall masked man with a breathing problem strangling all the good guys? And why does absolutely everyone have such terrible aim with their blasters!?

Some things I explained, and some things I told Maya to just be patient about and continue watching, because the context would be revealed as the story unfolded. Action is interesting, but we need context for clarity.

The good news has a context. When we read about Jesus' life and teaching, we're joining a story already in progress. So if we want to get a good grip on the gospel, we need to back up, zoom out, and put Jesus in his place in history.

In the story of God in relationship with humankind, Episode I might be called "Made by God, like God, for God." Episode II would be "The Chasm," and Episode III would be "The Old Ways." When Jesus arrives on the scene, we begin Episode IV: "A New Hope."

But first we need to go back, before the beginning, a long time ago, before there was a galaxy far, far away, or any galaxy at all.

3

BAD GRAMMAR, GOOD LOVE

What comes into our minds when we think about God
is the most important thing about us. . . . No people
has ever risen above its religion, and . . . no religion has
ever been greater than its idea of God.

—A. W. TOZER

Let's try a mental experiment, suggested by a wonderful Christian thinker named A. W. Tozer.

In your imagination, travel backward in time to before the beginning. Picture everything rapidly moving backward, undoing, and disappearing. Civilizations are now gone, and the Earth is formless and empty. Now think away the Earth, the solar system, the galaxy, and the entire universe to which we belong. Think away all the planets and all the stars. Think away all matter. Think away all light and darkness. Picture the "big bang" in reverse. Think away everything you can think to think away, until there is only a void. Now think away the void. There is no void. What is left?

When I lead workshop participants through this thought experiment, they can close their eyes and put all their mental energies into their imaginations. This doesn't work so well when you're reading. But I will still ask you some of the questions I would ask if we were walking through this together in person.

What do you feel? Many people report feeling disoriented, like a kind of imagination vertigo, wishing they could cheat and imagine something solid to hold on to. They don't like the feeling of being alone in the middle of the empty vastness of space.

What do you see? Many people see only dark. Infinite darkness in every direction.

What do you hear? Nothing. Most people have no soundtrack for this daydream. They imagine hearing nothing.

What do you sense is right in front of you? This is a hard one, because participants know I'm likely directing this whole experiment toward a "God" punch line. They may even believe in God themselves. But once your imagination has bought you into a pre-universe reality of a dark, silent expanse, then at that point sensing the presence of God or anything else doesn't come easily.

So I invite participants to recalibrate their imaginations in tune with what we know from Jesus. How would your answers be different if your mind was saturated with the gospel of Jesus?

What do you feel? Give up feeling as if you are suspended alone in the middle of the empty vastness of space. Space doesn't exist yet. There is no "there." And there is no "then." There is only here. And there is only now.

What do you see? Light. Pure spiritual light (see John 4:24; 1 John 1:5).

What do you hear? Conversation. Warmth. Welcome. The light is love, and love is always relating. As I've heard Dallas Willard respond when asked what God was doing before he created the world: "He was enjoying themselves."

What do you sense is right in front of you? In front of you and all around you is the light of unlimited spiritual Mind, pure Love, in pure Relationship. This is God.

What was God doing before he created everything? Thinking of you. "Even before he made the world, God loved us and chose us in Christ to be holy and without fault in his eyes" (Ephesians 1:4 NLT).

This is our Origin. This is our Source and Sustainer. Even now, "we live and move and have our being" (Acts 17:28) within this reality. *This* is the Force (not the midi-chlorians). The God who is pure Love holds the universe together (Colossians 1:15-17). We live in a universe permeated by and held together with ever-relating Love. Relationship is happening all around you, and you are invited into that dimension of awareness and experience.

BORN OUT OF LOVE

The Bible begins at, well, the beginning. Before the big bang there was a Big Bang-er. And that explosive, universe-creating Force behind everything is pure Love.

We were born out of Love.

The Bible says plainly that "God is love" (1 John 4:8, 16), and it is the nature of love to share, to expand, to create and sustain life. So the Bible begins with the story of God's choice to create. In creating, God expanded his own internal experience of love. We are the result and the expression of God's love life.

God is love. And love exists within the matrix of relationship. Love exists *within and between persons*. Love is *relational energy*. Relationship is the sinew that connects persons in order for love to move between them, for love is only love when it is moving between and within persons. *While there may be relationships without love, there will never be love without relationship.* In and of himself, God could not be "love" without some form of relational experience and expression being intrinsic and elemental to who God is. If God were a singular monad, he would have to create someone or something else in order to engage in and express love, and even then he could only describe himself as "lov*ing*," but not "love." Until another being was created to love, we could only describe that kind of God as *potentially* loving, then later as *actually* loving. To say that "God is love" is to say that within his very being is the ongoing exchange of love. Love is, as it were, God's divine DNA.

THE GENESIS OF US

So when God decided to expand and extend his love through relationships by creating us, the Bible records that God spoke to himself in the plural: "Then God said, 'Let *us* make humankind in *our* image, according to *our* likeness'" (Genesis 1:26 NRSV). [1] God is love, and therefore God is persons-in-relationship.

There are three ways the Bible depicts God—three "persons" God is identified with: God is Jesus, our Lord, who is also called the Son of God. God is the Father, whom Jesus talks about and talks to. And God is the Holy Spirit, whom Jesus sends to live with us and within us.

These three persons, manifestations, aspects of God, are never treated like three gods, nor are they just three roles the one God plays. They are three distinct personalities within the oneness of God. What at first may sound like simple contradiction or theological gobbledygook is actually pointing toward the most profound reality we will ever wrap our minds and hearts around. It means that God is inherently relational. He is community in unity. He is plurality in oneness. In Christian theology, we call this the Trinity. And this is what makes it possible to claim "God is love."

This eternal and abundant Love that we call "God" chose to invite more persons into divine relationship:

> Then God said, "Let us make humankind in our image, according to our likeness; and let them have dominion over the fish in the sea, and over the birds of the air, and over the cattle, and over all the wild animals of the earth, and over every creeping thing that creeps upon the earth."
>
> So God created humankind in his own image,
>   in the image of God he created them;
>   male and female he created them.
>
> God blessed them, and God said to them, "Be fruitful and multiply, and fill the earth and subdue it; and have dominion over the

---

1. Unless otherwise noted, italics within Scripture quotations in this book are my emphasis.

fish of the sea and over the birds of the air and over every living thing that moves upon the earth." (Genesis 1:26-28 NRSV)

All people, male and female, were made by God, in the image of God, to be like God, in relationship with God. As persons in loving relationship, we are to extend this reality throughout the world. Through us, God amplifies divine love into all creation. This is our origin, our purpose, and the context for everything that follows. This is who we are and why we're here.

Notice that after God speaks to himself in the plural ("Let *us* make humankind in *our* image"), the text reverts back to referring to God in the singular ("So God created humankind in *his* own image, in the image of God *he* created them"). This is bad grammar but mind-blowing theology. God is the "us" who is also the "he." This is the God (singular) who is Love (persons-in-relationship).[2] *We were created by Relationship for relationship.*

Look at the sun and moon and stars. God created the entire universe as a crucible for relationship with you. Suns and planets are facilitators, but not the final goal. *You* are the goal. God made you like himself so he could do life together with you. This means that right now, God spends all his time and energy on you. And nothing else. He has no hobbies. No distractions. Just you.

THE BREATH OF GOD

When describing the creation of Adam, the first human, the Bible records, "Then the Lord God formed a man from the dust of the ground and breathed into his nostrils the breath of life, and the man became a living being" (Genesis 2:7).[3] What intimacy! We are made alive by the very breath of God.

The Hebrew word used here for "breath" can also mean air, or wind, or spirit. We sometimes talk about someone being "the

2. Just a reminder: I am following the biblical tradition of using *he* and *him* to refer to God. This is in contrast to *it*, not in contrast to *she* and *her*. In other words, this is about keeping God personal, not about keeping God masculine.
3. "Adam" and "man" are both translations of the same Hebrew word, *ha'adam*, which is derived from the Hebrew word for "dirt." It literally means "the earth creature," or "the earthling." To be human is to be a mix of the dirt and the divine.

wind beneath our wings." God is the breath that fills our souls and lifts us up.

So let's expand our kite analogy. God is like the vast sky, and he has made us to be kites that soar close to and within the atmosphere of his own divine self. And we will fly highest when two things are true: one, when we are tied by faith to Jesus as our historically rooted fixed point who guides our flight and makes our soaring possible; and two, when we are lifted up by the wind of God, the breath of the Holy Spirit.

LOVE AND CHOICE

Love is expressed through choice, and in love, God chose to make us. He also chose to make us *in his image and likeness*, which means we also were made to be choice makers. As choice makers, we would need to be given an environment that required decision making, the ultimate choice to love or not to love. This is the story of Adam and Eve.

For humankind to flourish as image-bearers of divine love, God chose to give us choice, and that choice was no illusion. Real love needs real choice. And real choice necessitates real options, with actual motivations, genuine possibilities, and real consequences.

And so God made it clear to Adam and Eve how they could love him in return, and he made it equally clear how they could choose to walk away from his love. God gave his image-bearers every tree in the garden of Eden for food but told them not to eat from one particular tree: "the tree of the knowledge of good and evil" (Genesis 2:17). The name of the tree says it all. In a perfect world, Adam and Eve would have had no knowledge of "good" and "evil" as contrasting categories. When everything is "good," then ideas of "evil" and even "good" become meaningless categorizations. But Adam and Eve, created to be choice makers like God, were given the power to change all of that.

God had chosen humankind, but would we choose him?

SEPARATION ANXIETY

After God creates Adam and Eve and gives them all the trees of the garden of Eden for food, temptation comes to them in the personal form of the serpent. Consider the first words the serpent speaks to Eve: "Did God really say, 'You must not eat from any tree in the garden'?" (Genesis 3:1).

First of all, notice that the temptation comes in the form of a question. This is the first instance in biblical history of someone talking *about* God with someone else. The serpent speaks to Eve *as though God is not there*.

The serpent subtly plants doubt about God's intentions and even his presence in the minds of Adam and Eve. He lures them into a dangerous train of thought. The bait has been laid, the trap set. If Eve engages the serpent along these lines, Satan knows that she is on the path to training her own subconscious in a deadly deception: assuming the absence of God and mentally detaching herself from relationship with him.

Second, notice the serpent asks a rather silly question. The serpent feigns confusion and presents a question rooted in an assumption that is designed to be easily corrected. He is after something more than clarity; he wants the conversation. "Did God really say you can't eat anything here? I mean, did he really put you in the middle of this garden to watch you starve to death?" The question itself invites an immediate response to challenge the asinine assumption. But in so doing, Eve is now joining the serpent in acting as though God is not there, and has begun to open her soul to a kind of subconscious, spiritual separation anxiety.

Remember: we were designed to live in love with God. Divine love is the spiritual air we were meant to breathe every moment of our existence. Once we begin to believe the lie that God has gone—that God is distant and that we are detached from his care—we may begin to make choices out of panic and self-preservation rather than out of love.

We can't blame Eve for her anxiety-influenced choice to take matters into her own hands and eat the fruit. We do the same thing all the time. When we mistakenly perceive that God is absent, we take matters into our own hands and fight for our own survival at the cost of connectedness.

The serpent tempted our ancestors as he tempts us today: to walk away from the love life of God to pursue our own separate and separated existence. We chose then, as we often choose now, to forge our own path and put self ahead of all else. We chose and choose autonomy over intimacy. Ever since, humankind has experienced a kind of spiritual dislocation and disorientation. Like a kite that yanks away from the one holding on to it in the name of freedom, only to spiral downward to the dirt, human sin led to results that were and are catastrophic.

BRIDGING THE GAP

When our minds buy the lie that God is not with us, some of us spiral into a dehumanizing descent into narcissism, greed, and apathy—a kind of "anti-love life" that only *gives* enough to *get* what we want. It is this impulse that fuels most of the events that make up the nightly news. More often, though, we simply live acceptable lives of selfish ambition: not so destructive as to draw attention, but not so loving as to help God's image shine in us and through us.

There are others, though, who choose what some might perceive as a more enlightened path—the way of religion. Religion is our attempt to bridge the assumed gap between God and us. We intuitively sense that "the nearness of God is my good" (Psalm 73:28 NASB), so we take matters into our own hands to close the God gap. We build our bridge to God with religious rules, regulations, rituals, and routines. We go to pious places and holy spaces, all the while following meaning-making men who run the whole show for us.[4] Religion offers a way to get God to stop being angry or apathetic or just distant and to start wanting to be close with us again. But religion is lying to us, just like the serpent.

---

4. You will notice that when describing religious leaders, I will generally speak about men and not men and women; that is intentional. Since the time of our oldest records, religion has been overwhelmingly led by men, for men.

As we continue in the story of the Bible after Genesis 3, we read again and again about humankind's needless struggle to bridge the presumed God gap. But God is patient with us. Over and over, God not only tolerates but actually accommodates and incorporates our various demands for rulers, rituals, temples, and sacrifices—the hallmarks of religion—knowing full well that one day, God will make his message, his love, and his presence exceedingly clear by becoming *Immanuel*, which means "God with us" (Matthew 1:23).[5]

Though Satan spoke the first word in starting humanity's detachment from God, God will have the last word in bringing us together.

RUNNERS-UP

Now that we've zoomed out to see the context of love in which the gospel is set, let's begin to zoom back in to see what the gospel means. As you know, we are going to examine the gospel in thirty words, three words, and in the next chapter, one word.

The gospel can be at least partially summed up in words such as *salvation, reconciliation, welcome, embrace, rescue,* and *reconnect.* Yet as we read through the Bible, there are a few words that stand out above all the rest as summary words for the good news of Jesus. So before we move into the next chapter, let's look at two runners-up for our "gospel in one word" award.

In true pageant fashion, we'll start with the second runner-up before the first runner-up. And the award for the second runner-up goes to . . . (drumroll, please):

Grace!

The leaders of the early Jesus movement called the gospel "the good news of God's grace" and "the word of his grace" (Acts 20:24, 32). After reflecting on all they had experienced with Jesus

---

5. You may sometimes see Immanuel (a Hebrew word) spelled Emmanuel (which is the Greek variation). Also, it is an often overlooked theme within the Old Testament of the Bible that most of the religious institutions and rituals instituted by God were first resisted by God, but demanded by humans. Through Jesus, God says "Enough!" See chapter 10 for more on this.

and all they had learned from him, this word—*grace*—seemed to sum it all up.

Grace means "gift." Grace says that God has already done for us everything we've been trying to accomplish for ourselves through our best behavior and our boring religion. Grace means that God offers us salvation, life, and love as a gift, free of charge, no strings attached. Grace is God's great end run around religion—the rules, regulations, rituals, routines, the holy men and holy means, the holy places and holy spaces—in order to love us directly and intimately, in unmediated closeness.

When I'm talking to someone who sees Jesus as an icon of religion—as just another founder of a system of religious rule keeping and holy hoop jumping—I become excited to share with that person the implications of the fact that the message of Jesus is "the good news of God's grace."

But while the first friends of Jesus and early Christian leaders used the word *grace* more than almost any other when reflecting back on all that God had done for them through Christ, Jesus himself used a different word to summarize the gospel.

This brings us to the first runner-up for the gospel in one word. If you read through the teachings of Jesus, you will notice that one word leaps off the tip of his tongue more than any other when talking about the gospel. In fact, while the Bible never records Jesus using the word *grace*, it does record him using this word more than one hundred times.

The word is *kingdom*.

Jesus regularly referred to his gospel as "the good news about the kingdom" (e.g., Matthew 24:14) and so did other early church leaders (e.g., Acts 8:12; 28:31). Kingdom can be one of the most misunderstood concepts in the teaching of Jesus. It has been misused to justify the use of force to set up something earthly, geographical, and political.

Yet Jesus never spoke about his kingdom in geographical or political terms. The kingdom Jesus proclaimed was and is a kingdom that exists within us and between us. A kingdom is more than a place where a king lives. It is a relational realm, a way of living together, with shared purpose, values, and loyalty, all brought together under the authority and care of the one rightful ruler. To say that the gospel is about the kingdom of God is to say that it is about God guiding us into a way of living together in unity, harmony, and purpose.

But we're getting ahead of ourselves. Later in the book we will return to the beauty toward which the words *grace* and *kingdom* point. For now, we need to move on from the runners-up to the one word that best summarizes the gospel.

So what could be a better choice than *grace* or *kingdom*?

That's what the next chapter is about. And, interestingly enough, the answer lies way back in Genesis, where we started. When Adam and Eve sinned, God planted a prophecy in the middle of the whole mess. God told the serpent:

> And I will put enmity
> between you and the woman,
> and between your offspring and hers;
> he will crush your head,
> and you will strike his heel. (Genesis 3:15)

One day, said God to the serpent, you will attack the offspring of Eve. But that will be your last mistake, for he will crush your skull. One day, the lie of God's distance and disinterest will be conquered by the truth of God's unmistakable presence and passion for humankind. Truth will come in person.

This prophecy is the gospel in seed form—what theologians call the *protoevangelium*, or the "proto-gospel." It is the good news in the form of pure promise.

God watered this seed through the centuries, showing glimpses of the gospel to the world. Until one day, in a small town in Israel, an angel appeared to a young woman with a wonderful message: *It's time.*

4

THE GOOD NEWS
IN ONE WORD

When we see Jesus, we see what God is like.
—ALAN HIRSCH

When I was young, I wondered why Jesus didn't come to earth as a woman (they seemed smarter to me). I also wondered why Jesus hadn't come as an Irishman (our family is part Irish), or even as a three-toed sloth (my favorite animal). And why had he come only once, so long ago, instead of coming today and every day for a visit?

My dad was a gentle, gracious, and wise man. I often peppered him with my weird and wonder-full questions, and he would patiently help me think through possible answers.

"Why did Jesus not come as a woman?" I'd ask him.

"He could have," my dad would say. "God can do anything. But men were the powerful people in that culture, as in most, and maybe Jesus came in that form in order to teach the people with power how to lay it down. Remember him teaching his disciples to wash feet? In that culture, a job like that was reserved for servants or women, who had no power. But as Jesus washed his all-male disciples' feet, he told them they needed to learn how to wash feet too!"

"Why not an Irishman?" I'd probe.

"He could have. God can do anything. But he had already been patiently working with a group of people, the Jewish people, to teach them how to be the light of the world together. When they weren't lighting up the world the way God wanted, Jesus came specifically to them, as one of them."

"Why not a three-toed sloth?" I'd ask.

"He could have," my dad would say, somehow still patient. "God can do anything. Back in the days of Moses, God became a fire in a bush and a pillar of cloud, so I'm sure he could become a three-toed sloth if he wanted to. But remember, of all creatures, we alone are made in the image and likeness of God. We were put in charge of the planet in order to take care of creation. Just think of it—through our choices, we can take care of three-toed sloths, or harm them by harming their environment. Our choices affect them in ways their choices will never affect us, just as our environmental decisions affect the lives of every species in ways that their decisions do not. We are the powerful ones in nature. But as we learned from Spider-Man, 'With great power comes great responsibility.' We are made like God, which means that we need to learn from God how to use power to love, to care, and to cultivate."

"But why then and not now?" I'd say.

"He could have. God can do anything. But his timing does seem perfect. Back then, Roman roads had only recently made it possible for the gospel to travel far and wide with new directness. The *Pax Romana* (Roman peace) made it possible to travel those roads with reasonable safety. And a common language, Greek, started to be spoken among different people groups, allowing them to communicate with each other as never before. Once that was all in place, why wait another day?"

"Why not just come every day?"

"He could do that," my dad would say, still with a patient grin. "God can do anything. In fact, he does that every day and every moment through his Holy Spirit. But Brux, if God was really going to become one of us—I mean, *really* become human—then that means he doesn't get to come every day in every place. Humans don't live that way. Humans live one life in one place at a time. And God decided to become human just like us."

My dad and my mom and my older sisters and Sunday school teachers and youth pastors—all of them had to put up with my many questions. And their patience paid off. I finally got it: God came to us as one of us. That's the incarnation, and it's central to the gospel. This idea of incarnation has profound implications. Theologians call this "the scandal of particularity."

In becoming human, God became particular, a specific human, not just humanity as some generalized concept. And that creates particularity in time and space, gender and race. God became this and not that. God became a man and not a woman. God became a Jew and not a Gentile. God became an Israelite and not a Canadian. God became a poor person and not a rich person. God became a first-century person and not a twenty-first-century person.

So if you haven't figured it out by now, I won't keep you in suspense any longer. What is the gospel in one word? (May I have the envelope, please?)

Simple. It's *Jesus*.

THE MEDIUM IS THE MESSAGE

One of the most fascinating aspects of the good news message that Jesus preached is that he centered his message on one essential element: himself.

Jesus was God's messenger, and yet he was more than that. Jesus was both God's *messenger* and God's *message*. Christ's closest followers were convinced that he not only proclaimed the word of God but *was* the Word of God. According to Jesus and his first followers, the messenger and the message are one. Jesus is the Word of God come to us in the flesh (John 1:1, 14). The medium is truly the message.

Yes, the gospel is a universal message that transcends any historical context or culture. This means that the message of Jesus can apply to any person of any time and any place. But the origin and substance of the gospel is rooted in a specific person, at a specific time, in a specific place. There is no gospel without the historical life, teachings, death, resurrection, and return of Jesus.

This is different from, say, the spirituality of the Buddha. Knowing details about the Buddha's life is less relevant to Buddhist spirituality than knowing Buddhist teachings, philosophy, and practice. And it is also different from, say, the religion of Islam. Muhammad was clear that he was a mere messenger and that people must turn to God, not to him.

In contrast, Christianity is all about Christ. Jesus didn't just claim to show the way; he claimed to *be* the way. Jesus didn't just claim to reveal truth or teach truth or point at truth; Jesus pointed to himself as the very embodiment of truth. Jesus didn't just teach a way of life; he claimed to *be* the very life we're looking for. His own words could not be clearer: "I am the way and the truth and the life" (John 14:6).

By claiming these things for himself, Jesus defines the gospel as this: the good news that God has penetrated history with his own embodied love through his Son, Jesus. Jesus becomes the hinge of history—the one who ties it all together, making sense of all that has gone before and everything yet to unfold. The apostle Paul spoke about "the light of the gospel that displays the glory of Christ, who is the image of God" (2 Corinthians 4:4). The gospel is a message that shines light into this world. It puts Jesus front and center so he can show us who God is and what God is like. If God is like Jesus, this is truly good news indeed.

The gospel is the story of a person, and that person is Jesus. This means that if you want to learn about the gospel, you'll need to learn about Jesus. If you want to become a student of the gospel, you'll need to become a student of Jesus. And if you want to read a book about the gospel . . . guess what?

You're going to be reading a book about Jesus.

THE STORY OF JESUS
The New Testament, which is the part of the Bible written after Jesus, begins with four biographies of Jesus. These are known as

the four Gospels—the gospel of Matthew, the gospel of Mark, the gospel of Luke, and the gospel of John. (Some scholars debate whether it is right to call Luke's gospel a biography or the first of a two-part history, partnered with his second book, the Acts of the Apostles. But let's not lose sleep over that.)

So here the word *gospel* is used to refer to four specific books of the Bible. Why is that?

The gospel of Mark, which most scholars believe is the oldest of the four Gospels, begins with these words—"The beginning of the gospel of Jesus Christ, the Son of God" (Mark 1:1 NASB). Mark doesn't go on to quote a pithy saying or sensational sound bite as the gospel. He doesn't teach an abstract philosophy as the gospel or merely point to Christ's death on the cross as summarizing the gospel. Instead, Mark goes on to tell the whole story of Jesus—his teachings, his miracles, his love for people, his challenge to religion, his death, and his resurrection. The gospel, in Mark's mind, is *the whole story of Jesus*.

Later in Mark's gospel, we read about a woman who poured perfume on Jesus as a way of honoring him. Some of the men who followed Jesus objected to her wasting good perfume. But Jesus defended her for doing what she could and added these words, "Truly I tell you, wherever the gospel is preached throughout the world, what she has done will also be told, in memory of her" (Mark 14:9).

Don't miss the meaning here: Jesus said the gospel includes this woman's story. If we reduce the gospel to a snappy sound bite about God's love or about Jesus dying for our sins, then this woman's story won't make the cut. Her story would be an interesting tidbit served on the side, like fries with a gospel burger. But if the gospel is first and foremost the whole story of Jesus, then her story *is* a part of the gospel, just as Jesus said it was. In fact, as we will see, the gospel is very much about these kinds of reconciled, loving, self-sacrificing, and other-centered relationships.

If the whole story of Jesus' life is the content of the gospel, there are implications for how we understand and articulate the gospel. We can't escape Jesus' centrality. This means that, while conversations about God are good, and discussions about love are helpful, and interactions that focus on peace and joy and faith are all wonderful, *until we talk about Jesus, we aren't talking about the gospel.*

JOSHUA 2.0

A disciple of Jesus named Matthew wrote one of the four Gospels of Jesus' life. In his first chapter, Matthew records the words of an angel to Joseph, the adopted father of Jesus, about what to name Jesus when Mary gives birth: "She will give birth to a son, and you are to give him the name Jesus, because he will save his people from their sins" (Matthew 1:21).

Joseph must have thought, "Don't I get a say in this?" Apparently not, because God wanted everything about this new human, including his name, to be part of God's word to us.

The name Jesus was a common name at the time but was also historically significant to those in the know. *Jesus* is a Greek version of the Hebrew *Yeshua*, which in English is *Joshua*. Yes, the name "Jesus" is actually "Joshua." Joshua was a hero of the Old Testament who helped establish God's kingdom by leading his people into war with their enemies. According to the angel, Jesus would be the new Joshua—Joshua 2.0—who would help establish a new kind of kingdom, lead people into a new kind of promised land, and save God's people from a different kind of enemy. Jesus would save us not from "those people" out there but from the enemy of sin inside us all.

So who was this Joshua 2.0? Who did his followers think he was? What does the gospel in one word look like? Let's look at three aspects of Jesus: as Word, Son, and Truth of God.

WORD OF GOD

A word is the most fundamental unit of communication. A single word, like *yes* or *no*, like *guilty* or *not*, like *positive* or *negative*, can change the course of someone's life forever. We use the word

word to refer to an entire message that has a singular focus. "I'd like to have a word with you," we say, or "What's the word on Bob's condition?"

After Jesus grew up and began his ministry, his disciples spent three years living with Jesus, observing him and learning from him. They became convinced that Jesus somehow embodied God's essence unlike anyone else. They saw Jesus as God's ultimate self-disclosure to the world. They didn't just believe Jesus *preached* God's word. They believed Jesus *was* God's Word to us.

Jesus is the Word of God wrapped in humanity. The apostle John calls Jesus the Word of God who "became flesh" (John 1:14), and begins his biography of Jesus with these stunning words:

> In the beginning was the Word, and the Word was with God, and the Word was God. He was with God in the beginning. Through him all things were made; without him nothing was made that has been made. In him was life, and that life was the light of all mankind. The light shines in the darkness, and the darkness has not overcome it. (John 1:1-5)

Later, John makes it clear the Word he is talking about is Jesus. The Word became flesh. The message became man.

In another book by the apostle John, Jesus claims to be "the Alpha and the Omega" (Revelation 22:13). Alpha and omega are the first and last letters of the Greek alphabet. In other words, Jesus proclaims his preeminence as the A to Z of what God has to say to us. Jesus is God's alphabet, the way God fashions his message to the world. God's ultimate message to us was not written through paper and ink but through flesh and blood.

This raises a big question that often confuses people, including a lot of Christians. Christians often refer to the Bible as the Word of God, but the Bible itself says that *Jesus* is the Word of God. So which is it?

Christians are eager to read, study, memorize, and meditate on the truth of the Bible. We learn all about Jesus from the Bible— the Old Testament (the Hebrew Bible) points to the coming of

Jesus as a promise, and the New Testament (that part written after Jesus) records his life and teachings, as well as the early history and thinking of the first generation of Christ-followers. The Bible is our best historical record of Jesus, because it was all written before the end of the first century, just decades after the actual events. Christians also believe it is inspired and preserved by God to help his people know how to live (see 2 Timothy 3:16-17). It makes perfect sense that if God was going to go to the trouble of incarnating himself into a human life so that at least some people could see and hear his message firsthand, God would care enough to find a way to preserve the record of that incarnated revelation for the rest of us. So it also makes sense that Christians want to read this record regularly and meditate on its truth.

But we do all of that not because the Bible is God's ultimate self-disclosure. We read the Bible because it is the best God-given window through which we get a clear view of Jesus—who *is* God's ultimate self-disclosure. The Bible is not a painting to be looked *at*, but a window to be looked *through*, and through that window we see Jesus. Christ-followers believe in the inerrant, infallible, and authoritative Word of God—*and his name is Jesus*.

In other words, Christ-followers are not actually "People of the Book," as the Qur'an calls Christians. We are people of the Person. We don't follow the Bible—we read the Bible so we can follow Jesus. There is a difference.

For instance, if I follow the Bible, I can use its stories to justify all kinds of violence, from beating children to waging all-out holy war. But if I follow the Jesus whom I read about in the Bible, he won't let me get away with any of that. In fact, Jesus won't let any of us get away with anything short of active, other-centered, nonviolent, enemy-embracing love.

Religious people throughout history have used the Bible as a weapon, and still do today. They parachute into a Bible passage, grab a verse out of context, and add it to their arsenal of hate. But the love of God revealed through Jesus challenges that approach at every turn. When we approach the Bible the way the Bible itself tells us to, with Jesus at the center, he becomes the ultimate context for every other truth we learn in those pages. Jesus becomes the lens through which we see the real meaning of all Scripture.

Some religious leaders in Jesus' day were all about the Holy Scriptures. But they didn't let the Scriptures lead them to Jesus, and Jesus often challenged them on this very point. They lived by the motto "The Bible says it. That settles it. I believe it. Let's do it." And that led to a belief system that made room for exclusion and violence. It was to them that Jesus directed these profound and stinging words: "You study the Scriptures diligently because you think that in them you have eternal life. These are the very Scriptures that testify about me, yet you refuse to come to me to have life" (John 5:39-40; see also Luke 24:27, 44).

Herein lies the beautiful irony: we learn *in the Bible* that Jesus wants us to move *beyond* just learning the Bible. Sure, from the outside in, we look like a People of the Book, reading and studying our Holy Scriptures like people of any other religion. But looks can be deceiving. From the inside out, we are a movement of people who follow Jesus, and that shapes how we read our own Bibles.

Read the Bible to learn about Jesus. Follow Jesus. Rinse and repeat.

SON OF GOD

Sometimes, critics of the gospel suggest that the early Christians made up the whole story—or at least the bits about Jesus claiming to be something special. Maybe he was a good Jewish rabbi, or maybe he was a kind of universal teacher, or maybe he was even a prophet. But he certainly was not some special "Son of God" in any unique sense that would set him apart from the rest of us. After all, aren't we all God's sons and daughters?

In Mark's gospel, Jesus rebuked the religious leaders of his day for their stubborn refusal to accept his truth by telling them a story. The parable, recounted in Mark 12:1-12, is about a landowner who has tenants on his land who refuse to pay their rent. The landowner sends a succession of servants to declare his authority and to collect his payment, but each servant is rejected by the selfish tenants. Finally, the landowner sends his only son to deliver his message, hoping they will finally listen to him. But alas, the evil tenants reject and kill the landlord's only son.

The story is simple, but it reveals something profound about how Jesus saw himself. Jesus cast himself in the story not as another servant or prophet of God, not as just another messenger in a long line of messengers, but as God's one and only Son. Jesus saw himself as unique in relation to God as his Father. Jesus did not believe he was just another rabbi or prophet or guru or teacher or spokesperson on behalf of God. He saw himself as someone uniquely qualified to show us what God looks like through his family resemblance to the Father.[1]

What is brilliant about Jesus is that we can look at his life and teachings and get a view into the heart of the universe, the essence of God. And that essence is gentle, caring, compassionate Love. Jesus, if we believe him, shows us God in a way no one before or after has done. As the Son of God, Jesus shows us what the infinite God looks like in finite form (see John 14:9).

I'm not a fan of puzzles, but I have friends who are, and one thing I've learned is that the picture on the box is an important tool to help us put the pieces together properly. Jesus is God's picture on the box. If we stare into him, keep our focus on him, and use the pieces he gives us, we can begin to assemble the puzzle of what God is saying to humanity.

The life and teachings of Jesus allow us to see clearly what we are talking about when we speak of "God." Jesus is the whole picture. Each teaching of Jesus, each gracious interaction with seekers, each offering of forgiveness to sinners, and each challenging

---

1. Note that this story is recorded in Mark's gospel, believed to be the earliest of the four Gospels. This fact pushes back against the conspiracy theory that Jesus never saw himself as anything but a purely human rabbi. This theory suggests that it was Jesus' disciples who developed the idea of his divine status over time and eventually stated it plainly in John's gospel, believed to be the last gospel written. Yes, there is development, but in style not substance. John's gospel states plainly what Mark's gospel says through story.

rebuke to religious leaders is a piece of the puzzle. We may spend our whole lives putting the pieces together, asking the big questions about life, and wrestling with the hard issues of meaning and suffering, but through Jesus we have a picture of where we are headed.

Jesus is God's limited edition.

TRUTH OF GOD

Jesus claimed not only to teach truth or reveal truth or point to truth but to *be* Truth. Jesus said, "I am the way and the truth and the life. No one comes to the Father except through me" (John 14:6). Jesus is the gospel—God's ultimate power released into this world. He didn't just speak truth; he *is* Truth.

Now, let me state the obvious, because sometimes the most obvious things get missed. If the gospel is centered in Jesus, then it is not centered in anyone or anything else. Something cannot have two centers; by definition that is a logical impossibility.

The gospel cannot be found in the life and teachings of any other prophet, guru, or philosopher. That isn't a statement of bias; it is simply true. You will find truth in all religions, but you will not find *the* truth of *the* gospel anywhere else. There may be similarities in peripheral teaching to be found between Jesus and, say, the Buddha, but the central message is quite different. Other great religious leaders in history may speak truth, and we can learn much from many of them, but they do not speak *gospel* truth.

There is something unprecedented and unparalleled in what Jesus taught and what Jesus did. Only Jesus gives us the evidence that God is love. Only love can lead to true forgiveness. Only genuine forgiveness creates reconciled relationships. And reconciliation with God makes religion redundant, because we are already reunited.

Like it or not, the gospel is all Jesus, start to finish. This uncompromising centrality of Jesus is hard for some of us to accept, because we live in a pluralistic world in which religious disagreements tear families and friends apart. For many of us, building conversations on what we have in common with others and diminishing any differences feels more polite and more respectful. Certainly, this is a needed skill and important first step. We do have so much in common with each other that needs exploration and celebration.

But there is something this world needs even more than commonality: the ability to love and respect each other even when we don't have a lot in common or even—heaven forbid!—when we disagree. Gospel conversations can help foster precisely that. Talking about Jesus as uniquely important can be done with grace and kindness—the very grace and kindness that Jesus himself modeled. In the end, if Jesus is the Truth—the key to understanding the heart of God—*not* telling people about this good news would be failing to love them well.

JESUS. PERIOD.

When I was just starting out as a pastor, I had the privilege of being mentored by an older, wiser pastor named Ted. Ted got permission from some of the people he met with, for me to sit in on and listen to their pastoral conversations. While Ted was helping others work through issues of life and faith, I was quietly learning important lessons as a new pastor. I'll never forget the lessons I learned one day when I got to listen to Ted's conversation with Julie.

Julie was overwhelmed. She had just recently started to believe in Jesus, but instead of getting more clarity, she was getting increasingly confused. She couldn't fit all the pieces of the puzzle together. "I thought Jesus would make everything clear for me," said Julie. "He seems to bring a kind of clarity and simplicity into the lives of others. Why not me?"

Ted asked some gentle and probing questions, and eventually the problem became clear. Julie loved Jesus, and because of her generous spirit, she was trying to bring every other faith system she appreciated into her love relationship with Jesus. Her spiritual thinking was a mixture of the teaching of Jesus, Buddha, stuff that sounded like Eckhart Tolle, Deepak Chopra, a dash of the Sufi poetry of Rumi, a drizzle of the environmental consciousness of Wicca, and a sprinkle of Hindu philosophy from her favorite yoga instructor. Julie was trying to complete the gospel with the messages of other prophets or gurus—pieces that were never meant to fit together. Theologians call it *syncretism*: mashing together different faiths to get the one we like.

"Julie, I think you might be trying to blend your faith in Jesus together with a few other faith systems," Ted said. "It's like you're putting together the God puzzle using pieces blended together from a few different puzzle boxes. And the more frustrated you get, the more you think you must be missing pieces, and the more you think you must be missing pieces, the more puzzle boxes you open and dump the pieces into your puzzle piece pile. No wonder you're feeling overwhelmed!"

A light was going on. I could see that Julie was beginning to get the centrality and sufficiency of Jesus. What she needed was not more but less. She needed to work on one puzzle at a time.

"Julie, I think maybe you're a spiritual overachiever," Ted said. "You are trying to live a life of Jesus Plus, instead of Jesus, Period."

I listened as Ted talked with Julie about how she was relating to Jesus as though he were *one* of God's messengers, *one* of God's prophets, *one* of God's self-revelations, and *one* of God's ways for us to know his heart. But that isn't what Jesus taught about himself. And if Jesus is wrong about himself, then we probably shouldn't trust him on any other topic either. Either Jesus is *the* Word of God, *the* Son of God, and *the* Truth of God, or he is dead wrong about himself—and probably wrong about a good many other things as well.

Julie's face showed an interesting combination of emotions: the joy of "getting it" mixed with the pain of still being somewhat puzzled (pun intended). Julie still needed help letting go of her syncretistic worldview, and Ted knew it, so he switched analogies. Julie was engaged to be married at the time. Ted asked her if she loved her fiancé, and of course she affirmed that she did. He then asked her if she was planning on marrying any other men as well.

She thought that was a silly question, and to be honest, so did I. Where was Ted going with this? Then Ted shifted the question slightly. "I know Tom is the only man you want to marry, but how about boyfriends? How many men do you hope to date on the side over the years while you're married to Tom?"

Again, Julie was incensed at the thought, as she should have been. "Why do you think it would be a dumb idea to plan on dating men on the side once you're married to Tom?" Ted asked.

"Because it would be deeply insulting to him and emotionally confusing for me," Julie answered. "Tom is enough."

Julie had just answered her own question. She didn't even need Ted to point out the obvious. Being an annoying stickler for clarity, however, Ted still said it. "I think that is how you are approaching Jesus. I'm not saying you can't be friends with other wonderful people, and even learn things from everyone you meet. But you have decided that it would be insulting to your husband and confusing to you if you tried to have romantic relationships with more than one person—and you're absolutely right. And Julie, the same is true for your relationship with Jesus."

Jesus saw himself as our "bridegroom" (Matthew 9:15). We can always learn wisdom from other worldviews, other belief systems, other philosophies, and other religions. But to be married to Jesus means that, in the end, we have decided that he is enough.

ENGAGING JESUS

If the gospel in one word is *Jesus*, then Jesus plus this religion or that philosophy is not a help but a hindrance. If Jesus is the gospel, then adding more to the message from another source does not enhance the gospel, but waters it down. When we borrow from other sources, we dilute the potent power of the gospel of Jesus. Dynamite plus particleboard is not really more; it is less.

Again, I'm not saying that we can't learn many good things from the teachings of other religions. But *the gospel* is all Jesus and only Jesus.

In the next chapter we're going to widen the circle to learn the gospel in three words. As you'll see, this isn't a different message. It's an opportunity to expand on the message of, by, and about Jesus.

You're about to learn the three most beautiful words in the English language, and the evidence that they are completely, verifiably, and powerfully true.

5

THE GOOD NEWS IN THREE WORDS

God is like Jesus.
God has always been like Jesus.
There has never been a time when God was not like Jesus.
We haven't always known this.
But now we do.

—BRIAN ZAHND

When you hear the word *creed*, you may think of a mid-1990s rock band or a *Rocky*-style boxing movie. But a creed is also a statement of faith, a summary of what a group of people believe. The ancient church had a few of them—the Apostles' Creed and the Nicene Creed are two of the most well known. Formulating a creed can provide an opportunity for believers to think through what they really believe, how they really want to live, and what they are really willing to die for.

THE FIRST CREED

Memorizing an entire ancient Christian creed might not sound very exciting, but you can do it, right here and right now. The earliest creed of the church was summed up in a simple, beautiful, three-word statement of faith: *Jesus is Lord*. That's the gospel in three words. (It's only two words in the original Greek, but in English we get a bonus *is*.)

By fully understanding and embracing that Jesus is Lord, we are transformed. Accepting this fact radically changes our understanding of God, which in turn changes our understanding of our world, our lives, our values, our identity, and our potential. All from these three simple words: *Jesus is Lord*.

The earliest Christ-followers clearly knew the power packed into this simple statement. The apostle Paul wrote, "If you declare with your mouth, 'Jesus is Lord,' and believe in your heart that God raised him from the dead, you will be saved" (Romans 10:9; see also 2 Corinthians 4:5). When we say "Jesus is Lord" because we mean it, and trust the Jesus story in our hearts, our faith and our speech come together to ignite our spiritual lives. That is salvation.

Notice that Paul doesn't call us to embrace the reality that "Jesus is Savior." He tells us that when we embrace Jesus as Lord, we get him as Savior as part of that package. Jesus is not just a means to an end, a ticket to get into heaven, or a way to "get saved." Rather, Jesus is our Leader, our Lover, our Lord here and now. And *that* is life changing while we live, not just life prolonging when we die.

When Paul talks about saying "Jesus is Lord," he doesn't mean that we just say the words, as if they are some sort of magical incantation. To the ancient writers, words were a sign of what was in someone's heart. So by saying "Jesus is Lord," Paul means that we are declaring where we stand and what we embrace as true.

Why are these three words so powerful? Let's break it down one word at a time.

JESUS IS LORD

We talked about Jesus as the gospel in one word in the last chapter, but there is more to be said. Why do we say "*Jesus* is Lord" and not *God* or *Father* or *Holy Spirit* or even *Christ*? Why is the key to our salvation the fact that *Jesus* is Lord?

To say *Jesus* is to acknowledge that we are talking about a real person rooted in real history. (Remember the scandal of particularity.) God actually became one of us. We aren't just talking about a cosmic Christ as some sort of detached, spiritual life force. We have vivid evidence, rooted in human history, that God loves us, literally, to death.

When the apostle John spoke about Jesus, the Word, becoming one of us, he said "the Word became flesh" (John 1:14). John could have used much more respectable words to describe what God became through Jesus. He could have said the Word became "human" (*anthropos* in Greek). Or that the Word became a "man" (*aner*). Or that the Word took on a "body" (*soma*).

Instead, John made a bold move to make a bold point. He said "the Word became *flesh*," which likely scandalized his first readers. The Greek word for "flesh" is *sarx*, a word so closely associated with our human frailty and brokenness that it is sometimes translated in the Bible as our "sinful nature." But John didn't back away from his word choice and the potential misunderstanding. He thought it was so important to help people understand that God loves us—all of us, in all our human weakness—that he said God became *sarx*. Through Jesus, God redeems rather than rejects what it means to be human. Through Jesus, God enters our brokenness, our weakness, our confusion and pain. God doesn't hover above it all like a deity whose glory is more important than his grace.

The strength of these statements by the apostles means that the gospel is not just about the death of Christ, as is often emphasized. The gospel is the whole story of Jesus, including him taking on our human nature. This is what theologians call the *incarnation*. Incarnation comes from the Latin *in caro*, which means "in flesh." Another form of this word shows up in one of my favorite foods: chili con carne. That is, chili with meat. So Jesus is, quite literally, "God con carne."

What's more, when we say "Jesus is Lord," we say a lot by what we are not saying at all. If Jesus is Lord, then Caesar is not, politics are not, power is not, economics are not, religion is not,

fame is not, fashion is not, appearance is not, food is not, fitness is
not, friends are not, and family is not. That is hard to admit. But
when we put everything else infinitely second and come to Jesus as
our everything, he sends us back into the world as better versions
of ourselves. The best gift we can give this world is to abandon it
for Jesus, so he can send us back into the world to love it like Jesus.

JESUS *IS* LORD

Because *Jesus* is Lord, we study the Bible as history to get to know
God's love better. And because Jesus *is* Lord, we can experience
that love right here and right now.

The apostle Paul wrote these three beautiful words—Jesus is
Lord—more than twenty years after Christ's crucifixion. If Paul
had said "Jesus *was* Lord," he would have been saying something
true but incomplete. That one little English word, *is*, changes a lot
about how we think of the gospel.

Notice how Paul ties together the truth of Jesus as Lord with
the reality of his resurrection. He wrote, "If you declare with your
mouth, 'Jesus is Lord,' *and believe in your heart that God raised
him from the dead*, you will be saved" (Romans 10:9). History is
full of examples of people who gave their lives in the service of
others. Only one came back to tell about it.

Because of Jesus' resurrection, the same Jesus of history who
lived and died in the first century is still alive and leading us and
loving us in the twenty-first. The resurrection is the evidence that
what happened at the crucifixion is really God at work and not just
one more terrible tragedy of history. The resurrection is evidence
that Jesus was not just one more innocent man killed by the powers
of politics and religion. It is God's great exclamation point on Easter
weekend. The resurrection of Jesus is why we can say Jesus *is* Lord.

Have you ever read a biography about a person long dead and
wanted to sit down with the person and get to know him or her
better? When we read the Bible to learn about the good news story
of Jesus, we are not just learning history. We are learning about the
person who is alive today and is with us and is loving us.

JESUS IS *LORD*

In Jesus' day, the word *lord* had three primary uses. First, it could be a title of respect, like "sir." English speakers used the term this way during the Middle Ages, a world filled with lords and ladies. Second, the word could also mean a leader: one who has authority. This is what a servant would call his or her master. Third, the Greek word for lord (*kyrios*) was sometimes used as a substitute for the name of God, *Yahweh*, sometimes rendered YHWH, what some people mistakenly pronounce as Jehovah. (I keep telling my Jehovah's Witnesses friends that they should change their name to Yahweh's Witnesses, but so far they aren't buying it.)

So what did Paul and the early Christians mean when they said the three beautiful words "Jesus is *Lord*"? And what do Christ-followers mean today when declaring this creed of the early church?

The answer is that we mean all three. Yes, sometimes people used the title "Lord" of Jesus simply as sign of respect (e.g., John 4:19, 49; 5:7). And other times we call Jesus "Lord" as a way of referring to his divine identity (e.g., Mark 1:3; 5:19; John 20:28; Acts 7:59-60; Revelation 19:16). But most often, calling Jesus "Lord" is a way of saying that he is our leader, our mentor and master, the one to whom we look to teach us a new way of living (e.g., Luke 6:46; John 13:13-14).

Why is having Jesus as our master good news? We humans enjoy the idea of being our own lords, completely autonomous and unencumbered by the need to submit to any authority other than our own desires. But it is human nature to be influenced as much as we influence, to submit as much as we lead. We all have to serve somebody, as Bob Dylan wrote. We aren't infinitely wise, so we need input from outside ourselves if we want to flourish. Learning from someone who is further along in the journey is how we grow in any task, talent, or character quality.

So we attach ourselves to people or things, even when we don't realize it, and sometimes we are hurt by it. Maybe it's a relationship that isn't healthy, a habit that is slowly destroying us, a pattern of thinking that is silently killing us. When we finally realize that this is happening to us, some of us try to detach ourselves from everything, like the kite that cuts its own string. But we weren't made for detachment—we were made for attachment to the One who loves us most and will lead us toward becoming the best version of ourselves.

When I say the words "Jesus is Lord," I am really saying that I submit to Jesus as *my* Lord. And when we come to that place, it really becomes good news. We can then live our lives attached to pure love, pure life, and a light that will overcome the darkness of apathy that plagues our world. To say "Jesus is Lord" is to say "Jesus is *my* Lord," which is to say that I am choosing to become a student, an apprentice, a disciple of the One who will mentor me in the way of love for the rest of my life.

So to say "Jesus is Lord" is to say that we affirm his uniqueness in sharing God's word with us, telling God's will to us, and showing God's way for us to live. To say "Jesus is Lord" is to say "Jesus embodies God to me, and because of that I come to him in order to learn how to live my life the best way possible." When we say "Jesus is Lord," we affirm that this figure of history is still alive and leading us today and that we want to follow him. We declare our search is over and our hope has found a resting place in Christ.

GOD'S HEART WALKING AROUND

To say "Jesus is Lord" is to say, among other things, that no one shows us what God is like better than Jesus does. Look at what John says near the start of his gospel: "No one has seen God at any time; the only begotten God who is in the bosom of the Father, He has explained Him" (John 1:18 NASB). This one verse says so much in so few words; it is dense with meaning, like truth syrup.

The first thing John says is that, until Jesus came, no one had really seen God. Now, the apostle John was steeped in the Jewish Scriptures. He knew there were stories in the Hebrew Bible of God *showing himself* to prophets and other leaders (e.g., Genesis 17:1;

18:1; Exodus 24:9-11; 33:9-23; Isaiah 6:1; Ezekiel 1:1). So why state boldly that "no one has seen God at any time"? John is making a profoundly powerful point: aside from staring into the life and love of Jesus, no one truly sees God, no matter how close to God that person becomes. Jesus is such a clear picture of what God is really like that every other vision of God is only partial, incomplete, and too easily misunderstood. Perhaps this is why the Bible says Moses, described in the Bible as one of the most intimate, face-to-face friends of God, really only ever saw *the back of God* (Exodus 33:23).

So according to John 1:18, God reveals himself to us definitively through Christ in a way that makes his nature crystal clear. God somehow gives birth to himself—the God within God, he who is in the "bosom" (literally, the lap or chest cavity) of the Father. It is as though God opened up his chest to show us his heart—and out walked a person! That person is Jesus. What we learn about God's heart when we look at Jesus is really good news.

This passage also says that Jesus has "explained" God. The Greek word used here, *exegeo*, is the same word from which we get the word *exegete*. Christian teachers sometimes speak of "exegeting" a passage of Scripture, which means to fully explain its meaning. Right now I am exegeting John 1:18 to you. And John 1:18 says that Jesus "exegetes" God to us. *Jesus is God's ultimate explanation of himself.* When we keep Jesus at the center of our seeing, hearing, and responding to God, we are seeing God as he really is.

Other first-generation followers of Christ put it this way: "Christ is the visible image of the invisible God" (Colossians 1:15 NLT) and "The Son is the radiance of God's glory and the exact representation of his being" (Hebrews 1:3).

Through Jesus, it is as if God says, "I know there are stories of violence in the Bible, stories of pain and of harsh judgment all mixed with stories of mercy and grace and healing and hope. I understand that sometimes you aren't sure what kind of God I am or how best to follow my will. You look to nature, learn from prophets and holy teachers, and flip through the pages of your Bibles and other holy books trying to find the evidence of my heart, to figure out what the great I Am is like. Well, it's time to nail that one down. Once you know my heart, you will be able to better understand everything else you know about me, in nature and in Scripture. Look to Jesus. This is my heart, my most intimate and ultimate act of self-disclosure. This is what I look like when I put skin on."

So again, why is this good news? Because if God really is like Jesus, then we can have confidence that God is deeply compassionate, scandalously gracious, and infinitely loving. We are created by, sustained by, and surrounded by a God who is Love. That is the universe we live in. In Jesus, we get our most clear picture of the heart of God. Because Jesus is Lord, everything about his life shows God to us.

And what do we see when we look at Jesus? A God who has infinite compassion on sinners and outcasts. A God who rages against religion. A God who calls us his friends. A God who enters this world not riding on a celestial chariot or amid a shower of thunderbolts, but humbly, born to simple parents of little means in a small town and without a place to call their own. A God whose warhorse is a donkey and who bends down to wash his disciples' feet. A God who is humble.

The gospel is the good news that God became one of us. And when he became one of us, he transformed everything every religion had ever conceived about the heart of our Creator and our own destiny in relationship with him.

The gospel is more than this, as we shall soon see. But it is certainly not less.

THREE BEAUTIFUL WORDS

If Jesus really is Lord in the divine sense of the word, then the implications are beyond encouraging. It means that Jesus shows us a view of God that busts through the claims of every other holy book, prophet, and preconception.

"Jesus is Lord" are three of the most beautiful words ever strung together in the English language. And they lead to another set of three of the most beautiful words ever uttered: "God is love" (see 1 John 4:8, 16).

At the core of our being, almost everyone holds a shared primary belief. For you and for me, this belief is axiomatic and foundational, a basic belief that we know we know. This idea resonates with all of us as somehow truly true, so that virtually no one would want to argue against it. To assert this proposition is to state what is obvious to our souls, to our deepest selves. And here it is: *the highest good is love.*

We will die for love. We will live for love. And we will give all that we have to gain love. No thing, no concept, and no experience is more sought after, dreamed about, or celebrated by humankind than love. There is no greater good.

At the same time, the very concept of God is, by definition, the highest good imaginable. There is nothing more great or more good than what we call "God." This fact is baked right into the definition of the divine. No one and no thing is higher in value, power, or personhood than God. Whatever God is, this omnipotent force is responsible for creating us, for calling us out of nothingness into somethingness, and for sustaining us as relational beings.

God is the highest good conceived. Love is the highest good achieved. So here are three beautiful words that bring together the two most axiomatic beliefs ever to enter the human psyche: *God is love.* We all intuit this truth, even if we don't have immediate evidence in the world around us to prove it.

And while most people want to believe that God is love, only Jesus gives us the historical evidence that this is true. Because we have record of the life of Jesus, and because we believe that Jesus is Lord, we can now assert with confidence that God is love.

LEADER, MASTER, MENTOR, KING

I mentioned earlier that the statement "Jesus is Lord" points not only to the deity of Jesus but also to his role as our leader, our master, our mentor. This is also part of the good news. When we realize who Jesus is, we can trust him to show us a better way of living.

To call Jesus our Lord is a way of saying that we follow him, that he leads us. That's why I tend to call myself a "Christ-follower" more often than I call myself a "Christian." Jesus also called his followers "disciples," which means students, learners, and apprentices. We sometimes think that Jesus only had twelve disciples, and that is partially true. He had twelve friends whom he personally trained and commissioned to become apostles (meaning "sent ones") who would lead his followers. But all his followers were and are disciples, students of Jesus (see Matthew 28:18-20; Acts 14:21).

So to say that Jesus is Lord is to say that Jesus is the one I look to in order to learn how to live. Jesus not only shows us a God who is Love; he teaches us how to live life while immersed in his love. Jesus' way of life is ethically revolutionary. Although the ethics of Jesus are not the focus of this book, it's important to say that embracing Jesus as our Lord gives our lives a new focus, a new purpose, a new sense of belonging and behaving according to a new love ethic. This love ethic is revolutionary and unparalleled in religious or philosophical history.

Inherent in the fact that Jesus is Lord is the idea that Jesus is our king. When we embrace the way of Jesus, we are choosing to be part of his kingdom. Jesus is Lord over a people, a new community, living in a new way. Jesus called this the "good news of the kingdom." It was his way of saying that he was calling people into a whole new realm of life. A kingdom is a way of living. It is a realm, a dimension of life where our relationships are reoriented within a new framework. (We'll look at this in more depth in chapter 9.)

When I embrace Jesus as Lord, I wake up in the morning in a new world—a world that is permeated with love, where I am specifically and meaningfully delighted in by the Divine. And I wake up with a clarity of identity and purpose—I am God's dearly loved child, meant to learn from Jesus so I can love like Jesus.

THE JESUS FILTER

Knowing that Jesus is Lord also helps me boil down the most important truth from a variety of sources.

Do I always interpret passages I read in the Bible correctly? The odds are against it. But one thing that helps me be more accurate is always comparing everything I read in the Bible to what I know about *Jesus* from the Bible. Does my interpretation of a particular verse or story line up with the life, teachings, and character of Christ? If so, I'm probably on the right track. If not, I need to rethink my interpretation.

Has every teaching of the Christian church been in line with the teaching of Jesus? Far from it. So the "Jesus filter" helps me discern when the church itself is getting off course.

What should I do, for example, when I hear religious people project meaning onto various life events, natural disasters, and relational challenges? "God sent that hurricane to punish sinners." "Your cancer must be God sending you a message." "You didn't get that promotion because you didn't envision it, claim it, and project it into the universe." "Your suffering is God's way of helping you burn off your bad karma."

When I hear things like this, I can again ask the question, is this in line with what I know about Jesus? Because if it isn't, then it's unlikely that these ideas are showing me God's heart. Rather than look for God in any one disaster, for instance, I look for God's heart in the ways people are responding to the disaster, bringing help and healing to the sick, or offering comfort to the bereaved. Because I believe Jesus is Lord, I submit every religious idea, every philosophical notion, and every ethical option to his leadership.

Jesus said, "All authority in heaven and on earth has been given to *me*" (Matthew 28:18). When we give spiritual authority to anything or anyone else, even the Bible itself, we can justify almost anything. Jesus went on to say that the most important thing is to help people become followers of him, disciples of Jesus, students of his way, "teaching them to obey everything *I* have commanded you" (Matthew 28:20). This could have been the perfect opportunity for Jesus to say that we should teach people how to follow "everything the Bible commands" or "everything their heart tells them" or "whatever the church declares." But Jesus said that becoming a Christ-follower is about following Christ, his teachings, his example, his will, and his way.

When religious people talk about God having authority in their lives, I hope they are naturally kind people. Because anyone can use "God" to justify almost anything. And when they talk about the Bible as their sole authority, that doesn't make me any more comfortable, because again, the Bible can be and has been used to justify almost any behavior.

Because Jesus is Lord and has all authority in heaven and on earth, and because being a Christian is about living out *his* teaching, then Christ-followers really are good news people.

OTHELLO REVISITED

You have arrived at a hinge in this book. If you have read from the beginning and you want to keep going, you are already going beyond just getting a good introduction to the gospel. You are becoming a student of the good news.

If you feel satiated, this would be a fine place to bow out and know that you've learned the basics of the message and mission of Jesus. You already know the gospel as summarized in one and three words.

But now it's time to take it up a notch and pursue a more advanced understanding. The rest of this book is composed of a deeper exploration of the good news, based on a thirty-word summary. Remember to think of these one-, three-, and thirty-word summaries as concentric circles. You will find everything you've learned so far within the "the gospel in thirty words." So this further exploration will be both review and progress. There *will* be repetition, but at different levels of detail.

In the following chapters you're going to learn about:

- *the ground of the gospel*: everything the gospel is based on, the *who* at the heart of the good news (and if you've been paying attention, you already know who this is!);
- *the gifts of the gospel*: those things Jesus has accomplished for us and offers to us; and
- *the goal of the gospel*: the *why* behind the *what* of it all.

Remember the slogan for the board game Othello? "A minute to learn, a lifetime to master." Now you have taken more than a few minutes to learn the basics of the gospel. If this is all you read or all you remember from this book, it is enough. It's that simple.

But I hope you will read on—not because you have to, but because you want to. Because the gospel is the message of God to us, it has a beautiful simplicity *and* an inexhaustible intricacy. It's so simple a child can grasp it and so rich you can spend the rest of your life studying it.

PART II

6

THE GOOD NEWS
IN THIRTY WORDS

*To him who loves us and has freed us from our sins by his blood,
and has made us to be a kingdom and priests to serve his God
and Father—to him be glory and power for ever and ever! Amen.*
—THE APOSTLE JOHN

Have you ever had two wonderful friends you love but who don't know each other? Usually you can't wait to have them meet and enjoy one another the way you enjoy their friendship. I feel this way about people and Jesus.

I like people. And I love Jesus. And I want them to meet and be friends. Simple. The best way I can help make this happen is to share what I know about Jesus with people so they can get to know him (since he already knows them!).

Because of this, over the years I have paid attention to and made use of different tools that Christians have produced to summarize the essence of the message and mission of Jesus for people. And there is no shortage of these tools. During the past few decades, evangelical Christians (literally, that's "good news Christians") have developed numerous summaries of the gospel to help them think about it and communicate it clearly. And I've made use of every one.

FIVE FOUR-POINT FRAGMENTS

Let's take a tour of some of the most popular gospel communication tools developed by Christians over recent decades. Each approach has some value and some weakness. Oddly enough, each has four points.

The first and most popular of these evangelism tools was called the "Four Spiritual Laws," written by Bill Bright in the 1950s and published by an organization called Campus Crusade for Christ (now called "Cru" in the United States and "Power to Change" in Canada). This is arguably the single most influential form of communicating the gospel in recent history. I learned these four spiritual laws when, as a child, I first learned about the gospel.

1. God loves you and has a wonderful plan for your life (John 3:16; 10:10).
2. Our sin has separated us from God (Romans 3:23; 6:23).
3. Jesus is God's only provision for our salvation (John 14:6; Romans 5:8).
4. We must receive salvation by faith in Christ (John 1:12; Ephesians 2:8-9).

A little later, another Christian organization called the Navigators began to present the gospel in what they called "The Bridge to Life." I learned this approach during my young adult years, and shared it with lots of my university friends.

1. The Bible teaches that God loves all humans and wants them to know him (Genesis 1:27; John 10:10).
2. But humans sinned against God and are separated from God, leading to death and judgement (Isaiah 59:2; Romans 3:23).
3. There is a solution: Jesus Christ died on the cross for our sins and in so doing has become the bridge between humanity and God (Romans 5:8; 1 Timothy 2:5; 1 Peter 3:18).
4. Only those who trust Christ can cross the bridge—the choice is yours (John 3:16; 5:24).

Then the Billy Graham Association created something called "Steps to Peace with God." So I dove right in, sharing this message with lots of people and even doing some door-to-door evangelism with this approach. (I always liked going door-to-door because I had fun with my opening line: "Hi, I'm not a Mormon or Jehovah's Witness, but I'd still like to talk to you about God.")

- Step 1. God's plan: Peace and life (John 3:16; 10:10; Romans 5:1)
- Step 2. Humanity's problem: Separation (Isaiah 59:2; Romans 3:23; 6:23)
- Step 3. God's remedy: The cross (Romans 5:8; 1 Timothy 2:5; 1 Peter 3:18)
- Step 4. Human response: Receive Christ (John 1:12; 5:24; Romans 10:9)

Eventually, some people noticed that these same basic points could all be found in one book of the Bible—the apostle Paul's letter to the Romans, using just four verses. So this approach to sharing the basics of the gospel became known as "The Roman Road."

1. Human need (Romans 3:23)
2. Sin's penalty (Romans 6:23)
3. God's provision (Romans 5:8)
4. Our response (Romans 10:9)

More recently, some Christians have come to believe that Paul designed the first four chapters of Romans to walk his readers through the basics of the gospel.

- Romans 1—God: God is the Creator to whom all people are accountable.
- Romans 2—Man[1]: Humans have rebelled against God.
- Romans 3—Christ: God's solution to humanity's sin is the sacrificial death and resurrection of Jesus.

---

1. Ya, the most popular versions of this approach say "man," not "humans" or "us." I guess women are off the hook.

- Romans 4—Response: Humans can be included in salvation through faith in Jesus Christ.

I appreciate all of these point-form summaries, to some extent. Because the good news of Jesus is such an expansive message, finding memorable ways to distill it into bite-size chunks can be very helpful for our understanding and our communication of the gospel.

However, each of these popular gospel outlines shares a common flaw: they are woefully fragmentary, reductionist, and incomplete. You can see that most of these summaries focus primarily on *salvation from sin* as the central message of the gospel. This certainly is an important *aspect* of the gospel. But if you're going to be a student of the good news, then you need to know and will want to share the whole message.

THIRTY WORDS

It would be irresponsible for me to criticize some gospel outlines as being inadequate and incomplete and not at least attempt to fill in the missing pieces. And that's why digging into the fullness of the gospel, including and especially filling in the commonly missing bits, is the driving force behind the rest of this book.

Now it's time to take a deep breath, dig deeper, and look at the gospel in greater detail. I want to give you a more expansive summary of the gospel, organized in a way that you can remember. We've already learned the gospel in one word (Jesus) and three words (Jesus is Lord). Now we'll look at the gospel in thirty words, and the structure of this thirty-word summary will form the basic framework for the rest of this book.

Here is the gospel in thirty words:

JESUS IS GOD WITH US, COME TO

SHOW US GOD'S LOVE,   **SAVE US FROM SIN,**   **SET UP GOD'S KINGDOM, AND**   **SHUT DOWN RELIGION,**

SO WE CAN SHARE IN GOD'S LIFE.

Catchy, eh? (And now we know how obsessive you are. You counted the words, didn't you? I knew it.) True, this summary, like all summaries, borders on the cliché, the memorable slogan, the snappy sound bite. We might be tempted to memorize and repeat this summary as our way of communicating the gospel. But that's not how I intend it to be used.

These thirty words offer a framework to help us recognize different aspects of the gospel message. They offer a way of remembering key elements and implications of the gospel. You can hold this thirty-word summary in your mind as a mental rubric for sorting through the biblical data about Christ's life and teaching. Used properly, I've found this summary very helpful in thinking about the gospel and communicating it accurately to others. But I never just repeat it as a slogan. I use it internally, to help me recall different aspects of the gospel in conversations or when I just want to meditate on the multidimensional message of Jesus.

Now look closer. We can break this summary down into three parts.

First is *the ground of the gospel*. Jesus is Immanuel, God with us. Everything that follows is rooted in this world-changing fact.

Second are *the gifts of the gospel*. These are four things that Jesus has accomplished on our behalf, for our good and God's glory: showing us God's love, saving us from sin, setting up his kingdom, and shutting down religion.

The apostle John summarizes these four qualities of the gospel message in a prayer of worship when he says, "To him who *loves us* and has *freed us from our sins* by his blood, and has made us to be *a kingdom* and *priests* to serve his God and Father—to him be glory and power for ever and ever! Amen" (Revelation 1:5-6).

Third is *the goal of the gospel*. God's goal is to share his life with us. God draws us into his very own love life, now and forever.

For the rest of this chapter, we'll unpack the ground of the gospel. The remainder of the book, then, moves on to the gifts and goal of the gospel.

GROUND OF THE GOSPEL

Look back at the definitions of the gospel in one word, three words, and thirty words we have covered so far. Do you see a pattern? For starters, *each one starts with Jesus*. This is no accident. All good news emanates from the historical events that happened around, in, and through that one divine-human life.

We can't escape the singularity of the solution Jesus offers. "I am the way and the truth and the life," said Jesus. "No one comes to the Father except through me" (John 14:6).

"But wait a second," someone will surely protest. "Why is there only one way to God? That's not good news! Truly good news would be the revelation that there are many ways to God, that every path leads to the mountaintop, and that it doesn't matter what form of spirituality we choose in this life."

This kind of thinking is fundamentally religious in the worst possible way. The "many paths up the mountain" theory is based on three faulty assumptions: (1) God is still up on the mountain, (2) it is our lot in life to climb up the mountain to get to God, and (3) the paths and the Person are separate. Nothing could be further from the truth.

First, the story of the incarnation, God becoming one of us, is the heartbeat of the gospel. God is not "up there" somewhere, but right here, with us and in us. Jesus said, "I am with you always" (Matthew 28:20).

Second, the gospel is the message of grace (see Ephesians 2:8-10): God has given us everything religion tries but fails to give. We don't have to climb any path up any mountain to get to God. We don't have to *do* anything. God has already done it all.

Third, if Jesus really is God come to us, then Jesus is not just one path to get to the person of God. Instead, *the Path and the Person are one*. This is the context for Christ's statement in John 14:6 that he is the only way to the Father: Jesus is the way to God because Jesus is God (see John 14:7-9).

If God himself comes to us, it makes perfect sense that he should say to us that *he* is the way to get to know *him*. Why turn to anyone or anything else as a secondary source of knowledge when the one who is Truth is right here among us?

KNOWING GRACE

Let's say you are at a party and hear a number of people talking all about how cool someone named Grace is. Then you find out that Grace is also at the party. Let's say you've heard enough intriguing information that you decide you want to get to know her, and all of a sudden Grace walks into the room. Clearly, the best way to get to know Grace is to go over and talk with her.

Religion is like a person at the party talking about Grace with everyone else *but* Grace. Sure, all paths will get you that far; you can get to know *about* a person from many people. But to really get to *know* someone and not just get to know *about* someone, you need to talk *to* the person.

You see, if Grace is just a *message*—a collection of facts—then you can get to know that message through anyone. Many paths lead to that knowledge. But if Grace is a *person*, then the only way you can really know Grace is through Grace.

So back to the party: there you are, trying to get up the courage to stop talking with everyone except Grace *about* Grace and instead walk right up *to* Grace to get to know her. Wouldn't it be wonderful if, while you were trying to muster up the courage, Grace took the initiative and came over to get to know you? Wouldn't it be wonderful if Grace told you she had been looking for you and looking forward to getting to know *you* all this time as well?

That's the message of Jesus.

Jesus says he is the only way to the Father, but then he adds, "Anyone who has seen me has seen the Father" (John 14:9). Jesus claims to be the way to God because he *is* God, and God has come to us. To claim that Jesus is the only way to God isn't arrogant, judgmental, or narrow; it's just stating the obvious. God is the only way to God. And he has taken the initiative to come to us to love us. In the words of the apostle John, "We love because he first loved us" (1 John 4:19).

Different religions may represent different paths up the same mountain, as the cliché goes. But God has come down from the mountain to meet us where we are. This doesn't mean that every other religion is completely false; it means that only Jesus is completely true. We learn from all but cling to Christ. There is only one path—Jesus—and *God* travels that path to *us*!

Most of us are familiar with the basics of the Christmas story—a star, a stable, shepherds, wise men, angels, and two poor parents who don't know what hit them. There are many lessons we could draw from the story, but one overarching reality shines through: God chooses to identify with the weak, the poor, and the hurting. When God comes to earth, he enters as a baby, at the mercy of two humans to raise and care for him, trusting his life into the hands of those he loves. He is a king without a palace, a master without slaves, a leader without an army.

Why would the Creator of the world do such a thing? Why would he enter into the world in such a vulnerable way? Perhaps God wants to communicate that he has come not to force us into submission from the top down, but to start a grassroots movement that will woo us and win us with love from the ground up.

IMMANUEL

Matthew, a disciple of Jesus, tells the Christmas story in his biography of Jesus, and in the middle of it all he comments: "All this took place to fulfill what the Lord had said through the prophet: 'The virgin will conceive and give birth to a son, and they will call him Immanuel' (which means 'God with us')" (Matthew 1:22-23).[2]

---

2. A reminder: You may sometimes see Immanuel (a Hebrew word literally meaning "with us God") spelled Emmanuel (a Greek variation). Both are correct. While the New Testament never reports people calling Jesus "Immanuel" as his name, it does record people identifying Jesus as God with us (e.g., John 20:28). We often miss the most amazing aspect of this prophecy (that Jesus is "God with us") because we are distracted by debates about whether the original word translated into English as *virgin* actually means "virgin" or "maiden." The Hebrew word in Isaiah 7:14 is *almah*, which means "maiden" or "young, single woman." And in that context, such a woman was assumed to be a virgin. This is even more the case with the Greek word used in Matthew's gospel: *parthenos*, meaning "virgin."

God with us: this declaration is at the heart of the gospel. Through Jesus, God has come down to us as one of us, entering the same human pain and suffering and sorrow and love and joy and hope that we all experience. God is really with us in our experience. He knows what it's like to be human. The story of the birth of Jesus makes my soul sit up and take notice. What we read about the life and teachings, death and resurrection of Jesus wins my heart completely. God is with us not only as in "being present"; God is with us in disposition. God is really *with* us. The story of Jesus announces to the world that God is *for* us and not against us.

I remember meditating on this phrase one time—"God with us. *God* with us. God *with* us. God with *us*"—when suddenly it dawned on me. God doesn't just love us; he likes us! He actually is *on our side*. God is with us. And that means God is with *me*.

If the gospel was a technique or tip for life, we could learn it from anyone, find it in any religion, and declare that there are many paths to God, each one a different expression of the gospel. But if the gospel is first and foremost a Person, then there is only one way to get to God, and that is God himself, who has come to us.

GET US INTO HEAVEN—OR GET HEAVEN INTO US?

The gospel is about changing us from the inside out, here and now, not there and then. It isn't primarily about getting us into heaven, though it may include that. The gospel is about getting heaven into us. The gospel is about how we can begin to experience a taste of heaven now, in our relationship with God and others.

Jesus taught his disciples to pray for heaven to come here, not for us to go there: "Thy kingdom come, Thy will be done in earth, as it is in heaven" (Matthew 6:10 KJV). In the last chapters of the Bible, we see the Lord's Prayer finally and fully answered: there we see heaven, called the New Jerusalem, coming down to earth, rather than everyone on earth going up to heaven, and a new world begins (Revelation 21).

Remember those four-point gospel summaries? Some of them come with a diagram that shows humankind on one side of a chasm and God on the other. A cross, representing Jesus, bridges the chasm of sin so we can cross over and get to God. I think the diagram has value, except I think the arrow is moving in the wrong direction. The gospel is less about us getting to God and more about God getting to us.

It has always been God's way to come to us. God made us as physical beings, and he wanted us to live physical lives in a physical world. Having us become pure spirit beings, living in heaven with him, was never his goal for us. He already had those; they're called angels. But God made this world, and he made our bodies, and he called it all "very good" (Genesis 1:31). From the beginning, God came to us, rather than make us come to him. In the garden of Eden, there was no throne where God sat, waiting for Adam and Eve to approach in order to meet with him. No, God came to them, "walking in the garden in the cool of the day" (Genesis 3:8). Life with God in this world, in our bodies, surrounded by our friends and his love—this is God's original design for our lives, and we shouldn't expect him to abandon it. Instead, he will perfect it.

God initiated making us, and then when we went astray, he initiated saving us. First he chose leaders, then he gave the law to show us how to live, and then he sent prophets to help us correct our course. Eventually, God rolled up his sleeves and came down himself as one of us. But it doesn't stop with Jesus. Jesus told us that the Holy Spirit would infuse our minds with the mind of Christ, reminding us of his teaching, convicting us when we stray, and encouraging us when we suffer (see John 15:26-27; 16:15).

In fact, I believe that one reason you're reading this book right now is because of the activity of the Holy Spirit in your life. You have never been without the Spirit's influence. He has been with you all along as a voice of conviction and encouragement, patiently moving you toward Jesus. This isn't fatalism. You were never forced. If you feel yourself drawn to Jesus, it was no Jedi mind trick. You have not been coerced against your will.

Rather, your will is responding to love. You have responded freely to the Spirit's influence. And when you choose to fully embrace the way of Jesus, the Holy Spirit will fill your spirit with his own character, giving you the power to change from the inside out. You will know that God knows you intimately. God gets you.

"I GET YOU"

Laura was a broken woman. Her husband had left her for someone else, and she was feeling as if the rug of life had been pulled out from under her. She came to me asking for biblical advice, pastoral insight, and spiritual guidance. I gave her the best I could, but one thing in particular that I said changed the dynamic of the conversation immediately.

"You know, Laura, I get you," I said.

Those three words—*I get you*—changed the conversation more than anyone could have anticipated. I had been through a similar soul-shattering time years ago, and my heart was breaking for Laura as she told me her story. I felt as if I was really experiencing her pain along with her, and I wanted her to know.

"What do you mean?" Laura asked, wiping away tears. I explained that I really did know how she felt, that I knew what her emotional world was like right then. More than that, I didn't just know it; I was feeling it with her in that moment. "You see, I've been through something similar," I told her. "I'm not just trying to sympathize with you. I've been there. I really do get you."

Immediately something changed. Any wise words of pastoral counsel meant very little compared to the sense Laura now had of not being alone in her pain. The apostle Paul counseled Christians to "carry each other's burdens" (Galatians 6:2). Although it's difficult for me to describe, it seemed as if I was able to emotionally get under the weight of Laura's pain and help her bear it.

You've probably had a similar experience, on either the giving or receiving end. No matter how wise or encouraging a friend may be, nothing helps you bear life's burdens more than someone who can truly say out of their own experience, "I get you," or "I've been there."

That's how it is with God. Jesus shows us a God who does not rule on high as a kind of detached deity, untouched and unsullied by human sin and sorrows. God not only helps us through his power and cares for us through his love; he relates to us intimately through his incarnation. Jesus knows what it's like to have strangers and friends alike misunderstand him, desert him, deny him, and betray him. He knows what it's like to go through financial hardship and relational turmoil. He knows what it's like to feel pulled in too many directions and to be tired beyond belief. He knows what it's like to be tempted by sin and to struggle not to give in.

Knowing this can radically alter the dynamic of our conversations with God. When we come to God in prayer, more than anything, we can now hear him say through Jesus, "I've been there. I get you."

GOD'S SHOW-AND-TELL

Remember in kindergarten when you were invited to bring something for show-and-tell? You got to bring something personal and precious into class to let your classmates see it while you talked about it. Both aspects were important. Just talking about something would lack the demonstrative aspect that our minds crave for clarity. And just showing something with no explanation would fail to point out its significance.

Jesus is God's show-and-tell. Jesus didn't just speak the gospel; he leaked the gospel. It came out of him in everything he said and did. When we say that Jesus is God with us, we are speaking of every aspect of the story of Jesus: his life, his teachings, his death, his resurrection, and his return. Let's briefly touch on each of these aspects of the story of Jesus to see how they represent the good news.

His life. By entering the world as a poor baby and living a human life with all its hardships, God showed us his heart as never before; he radiated light to all who would and will look (John 1:9). Because Jesus didn't just *preach* the word of God but *is* the Word of God, we can study his life to see vivid demonstrations of what he taught. Jesus taught practical love, and he fed the hungry and healed the sick. Jesus taught enemy love, and he healed the violent wound of a man who came to arrest him. Jesus taught a courageous love, and he took on the established religion of his day, turning tables in the temple. Jesus taught forgiving love, and he died praying for the forgiveness of his killers.

Looking at Jesus' life gives us a clarity that no other revelation, holy book, prophet, guru, or teacher offers.

At the same time, Jesus didn't just show us God perfectly; he showed us what perfect humanity looks like. Think of it: not since Adam and Eve had this planet witnessed a perfect human life— until Jesus. When we study the life of Jesus, we get our clearest picture of who God is *and* who we were made to be.

His teaching. As the "Word of God," Jesus was always teaching. We can read about sermons he preached (see Matthew 5–7), stories he told (see Luke 15), conversations he had (see John 4), and challenges he gave to religious leaders (see Matthew 23).

At times in church history, Christians have not allowed the teaching of Jesus to shape their lives. Sometimes Jesus' teaching fades so far into the background that it seems to disappear completely from the official faith of the church. Here are portions of two ancient creeds, both dated to around the fourth century. Both creeds lay out the basics of Christian faith in God the Father, Son, and Holy Spirit. These two excerpts are from the bit about Jesus.

> I believe in Jesus Christ, his only Son, our Lord,
> who was conceived by the Holy Spirit,
> born of the Virgin Mary,
> suffered under Pontius Pilate,
> was crucified, died, and was buried;
> he descended to the dead.
> On the third day he rose again.
> (The Apostles' Creed)

For us and for our salvation
he came down from heaven:
by the power of the Holy Spirit
he became incarnate from the Virgin Mary,
and was made man.
For our sake he was crucified under Pontius Pilate;
he suffered death and was buried.
On the third day he rose again
in accordance with the Scriptures.
(The Nicene Creed)

Notice what aspect of the Christian faith had dropped into the background by the time these creeds were crafted. What's missing? The entire life and teachings of Jesus! The creeds skip straight from his birth to his death: from "born of the Virgin Mary" to "crucified under Pontius Pilate."

Thankfully, since the time these creeds were written, increasing numbers of Christians have repented of any theological focus that ignores the centrality of the teachings and example of Jesus Christ.

His death. Jesus made it clear that his death was central to his mission. The death of Jesus of Nazareth by Roman crucifixion is not just a fact of history or a tragic end to a Jewish leader's life, but what Jesus claimed he had come to accomplish (see Mark 8:31; 9:31; 10:45).

There is a reason why Christians eventually adopted the empty cross as the symbol of their faith. Jesus taught that his death, not just his life, would accomplish something of cosmic proportions that would change the world forever. He made this central for his followers to remember, through baptism (a symbol of death, burial, and resurrection with Christ), as well as through the eucharist, or Lord's Supper (a symbol of our receiving the sacrifice of Christ on our behalf).

His resurrection. How can we trust that the death of Jesus accomplished what he said it would? His resurrection validates his claims and reveals the reality of his status. Because of the resurrection of Jesus, we have assurance of the divine origin of his message and mission (1 Corinthians 15:17). What's more, the resurrection of Jesus provides hope to all of us that this life is not the end, that death will not have the last word, and that God's love is more powerful than the greatest evil. His resurrection is called the "firstfruits" of what we can look forward to, a kind of prototype of our own destiny (1 Corinthians 15:20, 23).

And that's not all. When Jesus died on the cross, he forgave his killers. Was that just a trick to get them to stop their violence? Through the resurrection we get to see if Jesus maintained that disposition or if he was rising again for judgment and revenge. Sure enough, *forgiveness* is the ongoing message the risen Jesus told his disciples to preach on his behalf (Luke 24:47).

His return. Jesus told his disciples he would come back to take them to be with him (John 14:3). Ever since then, followers of Jesus await his return. In some sense, Jesus has already returned through his Holy Spirit, "the Spirit of Christ" (see John 14:17-18; Romans 8:9), and is present with us today (Matthew 28:20). But there is a fuller sense in which Jesus will one day come again to set everything right. For now, God has left us here because there is work to be done (2 Peter 3:9).

From every vantage point, when we look at the person of Jesus we can see that he is God with us. God for us. God in our corner. God on our side.

And what's more, through his life, teaching, death, resurrection, and return, Jesus shows us God's love, saves us from sin, sets up his kingdom, and shuts down religion, all with one goal in mind—to usher us into God's own love life.

7

GOD'S GRAPHIC LOVE

The greatest happiness of life is the conviction that we are loved;
loved for ourselves, or rather, loved in spite of ourselves.
—VICTOR HUGO

JESUS IS GOD WITH US, COME TO

| SHOW US GOD'S LOVE, | SAVE US FROM SIN, | SET UP GOD'S KINGDOM, AND | SHUT DOWN RELIGION, |

SO WE CAN SHARE IN GOD'S LIFE.

If you're like me, you have an inner skeptic who never sleeps. If I were one of Jesus' original twelve disciples, I would be Thomas, who has come to be known as "Doubting Thomas." I'm the guy who is always questioning, always wondering, always double-checking, always asking for evidence. How can we *know* that God is love? How can we be *sure* that the God of the universe actually wants to be in relationship with us?

Let's be honest: our world offers us mixed signals about what kind of Force is at work behind the scenes. Nature can be

83

breathtakingly beautiful, but it can also be stunningly cruel. In 1849, Alfred Lord Tennyson finished a poem called "In Memoriam A. H. H." that took years to write. In it he struggles with what looks like a contradiction between what he believes about God and what he sees in nature. He speaks of humankind as those

> Who trusted God was love indeed,
> And love Creation's final law—
> Tho' Nature, red in tooth and claw,
> With ravine, shriek'd against his creed.

In other words, while we may *want* to trust that God is love, nature is so full of death and blood that belief in God's love can be hard to hold on to. The same is true for human behavior and culture; they give us contradictory evidence. We live in a world where the words *child* and *abuse* exist in the same sentence; where "just war" is a prevailing theology for most Christians and "holy war" is a rallying ideology for other religious groups; where mass shootings, mass bombings, and mass graves are far too common; where racism is rampant and discrimination on the basis of age, orientation, gender, and (dis)ability is still far too frequent.

Is this really a world made by a God who is Love? And are we really a species made in the image and likeness of that God?

The mixed signals don't stop at the natural world or at the capacity of humans for inhumanity. When we look to the Bible, we have to be honest that we get mixed messages there, too. We find stories about God's interactions with nations and individuals that sometimes encourage us, sometimes puzzle us, and sometimes downright frighten us. At times God seems infinitely loving, and other times he seems excessively punishing. Sometimes he cares for his people with the intimate love of a parent, and other times he destroys the world with a flood, calls for the death of nations, and commands the ritual sacrifice of countless animals.

How can we know, once and for all, that God is love? How can God cut through all the confusion to show us most clearly who he is? We need a way of knowing what God is really like. Doubting Thomases like me need some assurance.

And so, to cut through any confusion, with absolute clarity, God demonstrates who and what he is once and for all through Jesus. In a now famous song of the same title, Joan Osborne once asked, "What if God was one of us?" To which the answer is, then we would see love, pure and potent love, embedded and imprinted in human history through that very life.

If this first gift of the gospel—that Jesus came to show us God's love—had a newspaper headline, it would be: Good News! God is like Jesus! Jesus' life and love are the evidence that doubters like me require.

BETTER THAN SCI-FI

I've always been a fan of a good science fiction movie, and the successful Alien franchise of movies is one of my favorites. In 2012, director Ridley Scott debuted another installment, *Prometheus*.

Prometheus, a prequel to the other movies, is based on the premise that humans were originally created on Earth by an alien race known as the Engineers. A team of human explorers eventually piece together the clues that point to our own origin, and decide to make the arduous journey through space to find the Engineers and ask them why they made us. When they arrive, however, they find out that the Engineers want all humans destroyed. The ones who made us now hate us. They despise their own creation and have decided, thousands of years earlier, that all humanity must die.

The movie doesn't explain why our makers want us all gone, but director Ridley Scott explained his theory in a subsequent interview. In Scott's imagination, the Engineers originally did care for us, but they became increasingly distressed by our growing aggression and addiction to violence. So one Engineer volunteered to take on human form and walk among us, teaching us a better way of being ourselves. He taught us how to love our enemies, forgive those who hurt us, and live lives of peace . . . until we crucified him.

Yes, according to this sci-fi saga, Jesus was one of the alien race who created us, and his coming to Earth was our last hope of salvation. When we didn't listen to him and killed him instead, our creators decided we were beyond hope and set out to destroy us all before we could learn space travel and begin to spread our poisonous addiction to destructive violence to other planets.

It strikes me that, as far as myths go, this story is coherent. It makes sense. This is the kind of reaction we might expect from any lesser god. If any god had become one of us and given us ample evidence of his divine origin and called us to the way of peace and we responded by killing him, I could see that god saying, "Okay, enough's enough. I gave you every possible chance, and now I see there is no hope for you."

That's what makes the story of Jesus stand out as uncommonly loving. He did create us, and did come to show us a better way of being human, and we did reject him and kill him. But in the end, Jesus didn't react the way the Engineers did, with strict justice and deadly wrath. Jesus shows us God's love in ways we might never believe if we didn't have his own life, embedded in history, to make it all clear.

So what does this love look like? What characterizes God's love, as opposed to human love? Let's consider several dimensions of divine love. God's love for us is ongoing, universal, instinctual, unconditional, active, humble, life changing, and personal.

AND NOW FOR A DEMONSTRATION: ONGOING

"Here, let me show you what I mean."

One of my favorite professors in university would often pause to demonstrate the point she was trying to make. Sometimes she would ask for a volunteer to come to the front to help enact an illustration. Other times she would simply draw a picture on the board. Either way, I was always happy to hear her say, "Let me show you what I mean," because I knew that things were about to get a whole lot clearer.

Jesus is God saying, "Here, let me show you what I mean." He is God's demonstration of his central message of love for us: "You see, at just the right time, when we were still powerless, Christ died for the ungodly. Very rarely will anyone die for a righteous person, though for a good person someone might possibly dare to die. But God demonstrates his own love for us in this: While we were still sinners, Christ died for us" (Romans 5:6-8).

Notice that this demonstration is ongoing present tense: God *demonstrates* (not demonstrated) his love through Jesus. Through Jesus—especially through the fact of his death and the manner in which he died—God planted a flag in history, a marker that can never be removed, a fixed point of clarity that forever demonstrates his love. The crucifixion of Christ exists as ongoing evidence of God's love for us.

The Roman soldiers drove the nails into the hands and feet of Jesus, and God loved them. The religious leaders of his day hurled insults at him, and God loved them. The disciples denied and deserted Jesus, and God loved them still.

BEYOND THE MEDAL OF HONOR: UNIVERSAL

The Victoria Cross is Canada's highest military honor, similar to the Medal of Honor in the United States. These medals are awarded for personal acts of valor above and beyond the call of duty. Of the thousands awarded to date, more citations have been bestowed for falling on grenades to save comrades than any other single act.

The first Victoria Cross of World War II was awarded to Company Sergeant-Major John Robert Osborn. The sergeant-major and his men were cut off from their battalion and under heavy attack. When the enemy came close enough, the Canadian soldiers were subjected to a concentrated barrage of grenades. Several times Osborn protected his men by picking up live grenades and throwing them back, but eventually one fell in just the wrong position to pick up in time. With only a split second to decide, Osborn shouted a warning and threw himself on top of the grenade. It exploded, killing him instantly. The rest of his company survived that battle because of Osborn's selfless other-centeredness.

I love stories of this kind of bravery and self-sacrifice. They give me hope for humanity and offer us all a glimpse of God's goodness reflected in his image-bearers. But no matter how beautiful that heroic act may be, through Jesus we see an even greater love at the heart of God. You see, soldiers who fall on grenades do so out of love for their friends while they are on the battlefield trying to kill their enemies. Jesus died for his friends, *and his enemies*, and for everyone in between.

In Jesus we find a love so universal and unconditional that it is almost unsettling. Jesus was not willing to harm anyone. Instead, he died to save everyone, including the very people who were killing him. That's why we can say, "While we were God's enemies, we were reconciled to him through the death of his Son" (Romans 5:10).

After Jesus had been betrayed and abandoned by his friends, then beaten, mocked, and tortured by complete strangers, while he hung dying on the cross, Jesus was heard saying, "Father, forgive them, for they do not know what they are doing" (Luke 23:34). That is the love God has for you.

And then, when he rose from the dead, Jesus didn't say, "All right, you had your chance. Now it's time for a little payback." No. Jesus rose again with the same message he proclaimed while he lived and demonstrated while he died: the message of forgiveness and reconciliation for every sinner, saint, and seeker (Luke 24:47). Through the way he lived and died and lived again, Jesus taught us to love our enemies, because the gospel is the message of God loving his.

The good news is that God is loving us now, no matter what we've done or who we've hurt. Live loved, because you are loved. The cross proves it.

DIVINE OUTLANDISHNESS: INSTINCTUAL
There is a kind of love that is instinctual, parental, and maternal. Except in rare situations, a mother cannot help but have a

protective and caring love for her children. When she bears a child, a mother gives birth to a profound love for that child along with it. This kind of love transcends choice. A mother doesn't choose to love her child in this way; she couldn't choose not to.

This is God's love for us. God once said to Israel, "Can a mother forget her nursing child? Can she feel no love for the child she has borne? But even if that were possible, I would not forget you!" (Isaiah 49:15 NLT).

Jesus told a story about a son who couldn't wait for his father to die to get his share of the estate, so he demanded his inheritance early, insulting and hurting his father beyond words (see Luke 15:11-32). When the shocked and wounded father gave the son what he wanted, the son ran away and spent it all on self-indulgent living until he had nothing left. When the son returned to his father to repent, the father didn't say, "You've got some nerve, showing your face around here again!" or "How dare you think that you can abuse me like that and still have my favor?" Instead, the father ran to meet his son, embraced and kissed him, and threw a party for him.

This is so excessively generous that it probably isn't good parenting, in human terms. There is no "tough love" here. But that is the point. God's love for us is so generous that if it were expressed in human terms, it would seem outlandish. His love is so durable that it cannot be broken or discouraged by even our worst behavior.

The gospel is the good news that God became one of us to show us his love. And that love gives us the courage to come to him, or come back to him, no matter how far we've run away.

NO SKILL REQUIRED: UNCONDITIONAL

When I was a kid and attended church with my family, I thought the people at church weren't very cool. Compared to people I saw on television or even at school or in my neighborhood, the people at church seemed a little more . . . well, blah. As I grew up, I realized what a beautiful thing that was. That's what church should be: a place where everyone is accepted, regardless of their "cool factor."

The apostle Paul wrote to one church, "Brothers and sisters, think of what you were when you were called. Not many of you were wise by human standards; not many were influential; not many were of noble birth" (1 Corinthians 1:26). He then went on to talk about God loving them and calling them to himself, not because of how above average they were, but because of how above average God's grace is.

Smarts, strength, and status: it doesn't matter if you have them or if you don't. None of those are why God loves you. Grace is God saying, "I love you, but not because of your attractive attributes." After all, if we can list the attributes that cause God to love us, what happens if we lose those attributes? God says, "I love you because it is my nature to love. That's right: you're stuck with me and my love. And I've made you like me, so you can love me back."

The Greek word for the love of God toward us revealed through Jesus is *agápē*. This is unconditional love, loyal love, love with no strings attached, love that commits, love that shows up and doesn't run away.

God loves you because he loves you. It is God's nature to love you. It is who God is, not who you are, that is the source of God's love for you. This means that no matter how much of a mess we make of our lives, we are loved. There is nothing you can do to get God to love you more, and there is nothing you can do that will make him love you less.

LOVE WORKS: ACTIVE

Through Jesus, God not only shows us how much he loves us; he shows us what love is in the first place. "This is how we know what love is: Jesus Christ laid down his life for us. And we ought to lay down our lives for our brothers and sisters" (1 John 3:16).

In our culture, we are surrounded by books and movies and songs that say that love *feels* like this or love *feels* like that. But Jesus shows us that love *works*.

If I see others in need and tell myself that I love them while otherwise ignoring them, I'm out of touch. That isn't love; that is mere sentiment, a kind of self-induced, ego-enhancing, internal propaganda.

On the other hand, if I actively help people in need but I do it just so I can be seen as loving, so I can boost my reputation, that isn't love either. It is using people for my own gain (see 1 Corinthians 13:3).

Love is the combination of honor and action, of valuing someone and acting on that sense of that person's value.

Through Jesus, we learn that love is not doing what makes us feel good; love is doing what *is* good despite how we feel. Love is not an emotion of attraction or a feeling of desire. Love is the will to work, to expend energy, and to give our life to others by laying ours down or by lifting theirs up.

This is not the love of pop songs. It is the love that changes the world.

I'm not saying that love isn't attached to emotions in any way. We just can't identify love by any one particular emotion. Sometimes loving someone well will mean *not* giving in to our emotions of the moment.

GOD ON HIS KNEES: HUMBLE

The final words and actions of someone who knows they are soon going to die are often embedded with significance. Notice how the apostle John records what Jesus did as he saw the end coming closer: "He had loved his disciples during his ministry on earth, and now he loved them to the very end. . . . So he got up from the table, took off his robe, wrapped a towel around his waist, and poured water into a basin. Then he began to wash the disciples' feet, drying them with the towel he had around him" (John 13:1, 4-5 NLT).

Just before Jesus was arrested and sentenced to die, the apostle John records that Jesus "loved them to the very end." The word for "end" here is *telos*, which means the end goal or consummation of something—the ultimate expression or the complete fullness of some reality. As one translation says, "he loved them to the uttermost."

When Christians think of the *telos* of Jesus' mission on earth, they think of the cross. Didn't Jesus come to die? Yes, that is true. But he also came to show us how to live. That, too, is an expression of God's love for us.

And so even before Jesus died for us, he lived for us, leaving us an example of God's love for us and the love we can live as we serve others.

So at this Last Supper, Jesus took time to reconfigure his disciples' understanding of the Passover meal, saying that the bread and wine were his body and blood and that eating and drinking them would be an act of remembering for all his followers.

But even before that, Jesus did one final act designed to show the heart of God to his people: he got down on his hands and knees and washed their feet. Jesus was their Lord, their Leader, their Teacher, their Master and Messiah. He never called people to serve him but rather offered his entire life in the service of people. While teaching his disciples how to lead through serving, Jesus had earlier said, "For even the Son of Man did not come to be served, but to serve, and to give his life as a ransom for many" (Mark 10:45).

If you had walked into the room where the disciples were having their last supper with Jesus before his crucifixion, you would have been hard-pressed to identify who the leader of this group was. He would have been the one on his hands and knees doing the job of a slave, serving the needs of everyone else in the room, and showing them how to love each other without concern for ego or applause.

And in this we see God: washing feet. We see a glimpse of what God is like: in a word, *humble*. A God who is not looking for slaves or demanding service, but a God who serves, a God who loves in practical ways. Our society doesn't often think of God this way. This is not a God *demanding* worship, but a God we *want* to worship and adore out of gratitude. Remember, this is the Creator and Sustainer of the universe showing us his heart in human form—on his knees, washing feet, loving and leading by example.

In the end, what God does for us through Christ he invites us to offer to others: "You call me 'Teacher' and 'Lord,' and rightly so, for that is what I am. Now that I, your Lord and Teacher, have washed your feet, you also should wash one another's feet. I have set you an example that you should do as I have done for you" (John 13:13-15).

FROG-KISSING, PRINCE-GENERATING LOVE: LIFE CHANGING

Unlike romantic love, God doesn't love us because we are so wonderful. He loves us. Period. And his love makes us wonderful. Like the story of the frog prince, God doesn't wait until he finds us attractive before he expresses his love. He kisses us, and that love transforms us. This kind of love is called grace, and it is amazing.

One of the ways parents love their children is to help them grow up to be loving individuals. Jesus shows us that God loves us just the way we are, but he also loves us too much to leave us that way. We are always better off for having spent time looking at, learning from, and being loved by Jesus.

The third chapter of John's gospel contains what is perhaps the Bible's most famous verse—John 3:16: "For God so loved the world that he gave his one and only Son, that whoever believes in him shall not perish but have eternal life." What an encouraging declaration of love and life!

In so few words, this verse sums up so much. God loved the world, the whole world, and everyone in the world, past, present, and future—that's you and that's me. And out of that love came the definitive action of love: giving. God gave us Jesus, his one and only Son, his unique self in our form, his heart of hearts in the body of a baby.

And how can we respond to this love? What can we give God in return? All God asks is that we believe, that we trust this is true, that we take the risk of accepting his love for us and allowing that love to change us. And change us it will. The change will be so thorough, so transforming, that it will be like moving from death to life, from perishing to rescue, from separation to intimacy, from loneliness to love.

GOD HAS A CRUSH ON YOU: PERSONAL

What would it be like to wake up each morning knowing that you are loved like crazy? What would it be like to move through your day knowing that at every moment the person you loved the most was loving you back, thinking of you, wanting to be with you, desiring to have and to hold you, till death and beyond? How would it feel to live in that world and to have that life?

We have already talked about the profound truth that God is love. Now let's make this more personal: God loves *you*. Phrase it however you need to in order to help this truth sink in. God is crazy about you. God has a crush on you. God can't stop thinking about you. God wants to marry you, to have you as his bride, for now and forever.

Maybe you already have someone like this in your life. Perhaps it's a friend, a parent, a pet, or a partner. You can use this relationship as a point of reference to better understand God's love for you, which is infinitely greater than even your most loving human relationship. While other people and pets can love us well, they can only love us in finite and imperfect ways. They can't always be there for us, always supporting us the way we need. Their love is not perfect, even if it is powerfully healing. Now consider that what you experience in that earthly relationship is just a glimpse of how perfectly and how infinitely God loves you.

In the Bible, God constantly uses earthly love relationships to help us begin to understand how much he loves us. He says he loves us like a perfect parent, like a dedicated husband, like a close friend, and like a caring shepherd who loves each of his sheep. In fact, to those of us who have wonderful human love relationships, he says his love for us is so great as to make our other love relationships "evil" by comparison (Matthew 7:11; Luke 11:13). This isn't to devalue our human relationships but to elevate our understanding of just how magnificent is the love of God for us.

Maybe you don't have someone like that in your life. Maybe your sense of loneliness in this life is sometimes overwhelming. Then you especially need to pay attention to this chapter. Read it again, and pause to meditate whenever anything stands out to you. Your understanding of your world, your life, and your value can change to the degree that you let these truths sink in.

If this describes you, I'm praying for you, that your mind becomes awake and aware of the powerful truth that the creative Force that brought this universe into existence also brought you into existence intentionally, in order to love you. Right now that same God is thinking about you, loving you, and wanting your love in return.

May you be able to say, along with the apostle Paul, "The life I now live in the body, I live by faith in the Son of God, who loved *me* and gave himself for *me*" (Galatians 2:20).

God loves you like crazy.

Deal with it.

8

SEPARATION SOLUTION

Grace is God saying, "I love the world too much to let your sin define you and be the final word. I am a God who makes all things new."

—NADIA BOLZ-WEBER

JESUS IS GOD WITH US, COME TO

| SHOW US GOD'S LOVE, | SAVE US FROM SIN, | SET UP GOD'S KINGDOM, AND | SHUT DOWN RELIGION, |

SO WE CAN SHARE IN GOD'S LIFE.

I was once asked to officiate a wedding of two atheists. At first this threw me for a loop, since I would have expected an atheist couple to opt for a secular ceremony. When we met to discuss the wedding ceremony, they began by saying, "Bruxy, we're so glad you're considering doing our ceremony. We've heard you online, and we really like how much you like people and love life. We think you would be perfect, except for one thing. Because we're

97

atheists and don't want to be hypocrites, we hope you're not going to mention God. Oh, and definitely don't pray."

I affirmed their desire not to be hypocrites (that was very "Jesus" of them!), and I assured them that I wouldn't want to make them do or say anything that didn't reflect who they truly were. Then I asked them for the same courtesy in return.

I explained that, as someone who follows Jesus and loves God and believes marriage reflects that kind of amazing love relationship that God has with us, I wouldn't want to be a hypocrite by pretending to be secular. I told them that it would be most authentic for me if I did pray, but that they didn't have to. I told them that I would talk about God, but they didn't need to believe it. I told them I would probably sneak in a little of Jesus' teaching because I basically steal all my best stuff from him, but that they don't have to follow him. Then we could all be our authentic selves together.

After some more discussion, they finally said, "Okay. We can handle that. But one more thing. Please, just don't talk about all that sin and judgment and hell stuff."

Now that was interesting. Why would they think a pastor would preach a sermon on sin and hellfire at a wedding? I asked some more questions, and the story unfolded.

Both of them had been raised religious, and all they could remember was sermon after sermon about how we are all sinners in the hands of a wrathful God, destined for judgment and bound for hell. This couple assumed that sin and hell were the core topics that any pastor wanted to talk about whenever he or she got an audience. Even though they thought they knew me better, they were still suspicious that I might just be waiting for my big chance.

Thankfully, the wedding went off without a hitch, and we were all able to be our authentic selves. I talked about the God who is Love and about Jesus who cares for us as a husband loves his bride. I also talked about the first miracle Jesus ever performed: turning water into wine at a wedding. That went over quite well.

Sadly, too many people have heard Christians begin their proc-lamation of the good news of Jesus with this point: we are sinners and on our way to hell. This is the wrong starting point.

MISSING THE MARK

To begin with the premise that we are sinners is to tell the story of the Bible out of order, as though it begins in Genesis 3—the story of the fall of Adam and Eve. But the Bible begins two chapters earlier, with the story of God's radical decision to make human beings in his image and his likeness, to reflect his glory and to care for all creation.

The truth is that we are infinitely precious image-bearers of God, and nothing can remove that from us. We were designed to be like God so we could participate in an ongoing love relation-ship with God. This truth is what makes our sin so tragic. We were made for something better than the way we have been treating each other, ourselves, and this planet.

I understand why some people don't like the word *sin*. It has often been used to condemn rather than to offer hope. In other ways, too many people have used it too sloppily for too long, to the point of becoming a parody—its meaning eroded in phrases like "sinfully delicious." But when we know what it really means and use it the way Jesus intended, sin becomes a useful word to describe a real problem that we all share, and it helps us see the vastness of the solution Jesus offers.

The English word "sin" translates the Greek word *hamartia*, which means to miss the mark, to fail to hit the bull's-eye, to be off target. Sin refers to any ways we fail to live the life of love for which we were created. Sin is being off-center, out of sync, less than loving. Knowing that, you should be able to see that you, like me, sin. We are sinners. We are not always living perfectly on target.

This is the human dilemma. We are fractured beings. There is a me who knows better and a me who chooses the opposite anyway. There is a me who resolves to eat healthfully and a me who still reaches for that second piece of pie. There is a me who resolves to get enough sleep and a me who stays up too late again. We say things like, "This will be my last cigarette, and this time I mean it." Or, "Tomorrow I'm going to the gym, and this time I'm sticking with it." Or, "I'm not getting involved in a relationship like that again. I know it's no good for me." When we say these things, we may really mean them. But we often fail to follow through. We are walking a road paved with good intentions.

This isn't how we were made, but it is what we have become. Sin is the word Jesus used to refer to our fractured selves. And Jesus came to save us from sin.

SIN SEPARATES

"We're going through a separation," an old friend said to me. I had just asked her how her husband was doing. They were one of those couples everyone wanted to be like—the couple who almost makes you sick with their puppy-dog love and perfect lives.

That's what we all thought, anyway.

So when she told me she and her husband were separated, I was stunned. I was so stunned, in fact, that my subconscious mind got hold of my tongue before the rest of me had any choice in the matter. "Aren't we all," I mumbled.

"Pardon?" she responded, her head tilting to one side as though my words were a puzzle on the table to be studied and solved. I told her I hadn't meant to say that with my "outside voice," and our conversation moved on.

Inside me, a different conversation was happening. (I later apologized that I hadn't been fully present with her, but sometimes this happens. Don't judge me.) You see, their surprising breakup was a human example of the "breakup" we are all fighting against, every single day of our lives. The separation she was experiencing was a microcosm of the separation that all of us as humans are enduring.

I mentioned that the primary Greek word for sin used in the Bible is *hamartia*, which means "to miss the mark." And that is its primary use. But as we dig into the etymology of the word, we see something very telling. *Hamartia* comes from two words: *ha*, a negating word meaning "not," and *meros*, meaning "to be a part of" or "together with." So sin means to *not* be a part of what we were meant to be together with. In other words, *sin is separation*.

You can see how the word *hamartia* eventually worked its way into archery to refer to the arrow missing the target—that is, the arrow being separated from the target that it was meant to hit. Sin is a relationship disrupter. It separates people, divides groups, and fractures our own minds. All of this grows out of the fact that sin separates us from God.

Sin separates: that's a basic fact. By adding incrementally to that short sentence, let's look next at the cascading effects of sin on us and our relationship with God.

SIN SEPARATES *US*

Sin is that force at work in the psyche of every human being that divides us one from another.

Because we are all affected by the virus of sin, we malfunction. Deep down inside we all know we were made for relationships. Yet we all carry around within us the impulses and attitudes that destroy those very relationships.

When describing sin, Jesus said: "What comes out of a person is what defiles them. For it is from within, out of a person's heart, that evil thoughts come—sexual immorality, theft, murder, adultery, greed, malice, deceit, lewdness, envy, slander, arrogance and folly. All these evils come from inside and defile a person" (Mark 7:20-23).

The qualities of sin mentioned in that list are relationally corrosive. We don't have to actually kill or steal from or cheat on someone to diminish that person's humanity. The behaviors described in the above passage are, first and foremost, attitudes of the heart. Each produces an infinite number of microbehaviors that continually, if subtly, drive a wedge between us all, making it harder to forge the kind of committed relationships for which we hunger.

So when we say that we are sinners, we are acknowledging both that there is something wrong in this world, and that it starts with us. The problem isn't "out there" in the air somewhere, making things go wrong all around us. The problem is inside us—and not just some of us, but *all* of us.

SIN SEPARATES US *FROM WHO WE WERE*

In the beginning, God-who-is-Love made us, male and female, in his image and likeness. Our wills, our wants, our desires—they were all in tune with love. Think of it: What would it be like to always clearly know the right choice—the loving choice—and to make it, every time, joyfully, because we want to, not because we have to? What if we lived according to our original wiring, finding our joy in making loving choices? Wouldn't that be a beautiful way of being human? And that was our original state, our intended humanity: living and loving like God, choice by choice.

Making the right choice was as natural to us as breathing. We didn't need to think about it, to fret over it, to worry about making it. We weren't even conscious we were making "right" choices. Letting love lead our wills was as natural and unconscious as breathing. What a beautiful way to be!

This explains why the forbidden tree in the garden of Eden was called "the tree of the knowledge of good and evil" (Genesis 2:9, 17). As we discussed in chapter 3, the point of that name was not that this tree provided helpful knowledge about good and evil, but that if we chose to go our own way and eat from that tree, we would be dividing our lives into those categories. We were made to love, and every choice we made up until that point was to love naturally.

One day we will be ourselves again—the way we were meant to be. But not yet. In the meantime, sin is at work in our moral system. Each of us knows the effects of it by personal experience and by looking at the world around us. Oh, to be reunited with who we were!

SIN SEPARATES US FROM WHO WE WERE *MEANT TO BE*

You and I were meant to be something more than we are. Many of us live each day with a suppressed sense of shame because of our failure to be who we know we should be, who we wish we could be, and who others think we are. We may feel like imposters, always trying to make a good impression. But why do we need to try to be seen in a certain light? What is going on inside us?

The only reason many of us don't implode under the weight of depression is because we envision a future that is better than our present. One day I will have a better job. One day I will have more money. One day I will be thinner. One day I will be more successful, more attractive, and more popular. One day, one day, one day . . . But what if you knew that you would never get a better job, or lose the weight, or make more friends than you have now? Can you be happy today with today as today? Deep inside our subconscious selves the force of sin is at work, making us fail at being ourselves here and now and then accusing us for that failure.

Jesus was a perfect human (see Hebrews 4:15; 1 Peter 2:22; 1 John 3:5). Not since the "naked and unashamed" relationship of Adam and Eve had the world seen a perfect person. And how did we respond? We killed him for it. We simply couldn't handle what Jesus was showing us. His perfection uncovered our imperfection, and sin made us feel shame for the distance between who we are and who we were meant to be.

But here is the good news: If we let him, Jesus will not only show us who we were meant to be; he will also help us become that once again. Jesus will reunite us with our true selves.

SIN SEPARATES US FROM WHO WE WERE MEANT TO BE *WITH*

We were designed for intimacy with the Almighty. God is relational at his core, and we were made in his image. As we noted in chapter 3, we were designed *by* Relationship *for* relationship. But sin is a foreign substance to love. Love must reject sin, the way antibodies help the body reject pathogens in our bloodstream.

The prophet Isaiah recorded these sobering words:

Surely the arm of the Lord is not too short to save,
    nor his ear too dull to hear.
But your iniquities have separated
    you from your God;
your sins have hidden his face from you,
    so that he will not hear. (Isaiah 59:1-2)

Notice that God is not actively ignoring us while we suffer in sin. Rather, our sin has created space between us and God, and it is clouding that space, making relationship increasingly difficult.

SIN SEPARATES US FROM WHO WE WERE MEANT TO BE WITH *FOREVER*

Sin is like a spiritual virus, and like a virus, sin spreads. It multiplies, and it infects. Sin isn't a static thing that sits in the corner of our lives like a paperweight on a desk. Sin is less like a benign tumor settled somewhere in our body and more like a malignant growth that will slowly take over unless treated.

So how much sin do you think it would be wise for God to let into heaven? What would be the acceptable level of sin for God to allow into the realm of eternal life? Should God allow 5 percent? Maybe 0.5 percent? Would 0.05 percent be okay?

The answer to that question has to be zero. When Olympic athletes are tested for performance-enhancing drugs, they fail the blood test if they have even a trace of these drugs. Their blood is either clean or not clean. The standard for passing is 0 percent of banned substances. They can't protest, "But I only have traces of the banned substances, so obviously I don't use them too much." The standard is perfection.

When someone wants to donate blood, the blood bank must ensure that the donor's blood is completely free from various things, like HIV. The person cannot protest, "But my blood is *mostly* HIV-free, and certainly I'm not doing as bad as some people who have full-blown AIDS, so what's the problem?" The standard has to be absolute purity, and for good reason.

The same is true for our relationship with God. God's standard for heaven must be sinless perfection, just as Adam and Eve were when they were first created. Just being a *comparatively* good person is not good enough. If God were to let us all into the eternal dimension with sin still a part of our spiritual makeup, we would pollute the realm of heaven, starting the whole mess of planet Earth all over again. So God bans sin from heaven. He quarantines the infection and the infected to a different realm. Hell is God's quarantine solution for people who prefer to hold on to their sin rather than accept Christ's cleansing.

But that doesn't necessarily mean that hell is an eternity of torture, the way some medieval artists depicted it and some contemporary preachers promulgate it. Committed Christians hold different theories about the nature of hell. Some Christians see it as eternal conscious torment, while others see hell as a place of temporary punishment for unforgiven sins so that eventually people will turn to Christ and be saved out of hell postmortem. Still others see hell as the final death, the end of our souls. Just as physical fire destroys physical things, so spiritual fire symbolizes the end of spiritual things. Spiritual fire burns up, obliterates the soul. Hell is nothingness. No-thingness.[1]

There's a lot more to say about hell, but we'll save that conversation for a different book. In the end, the nature of hell is not a key concept when it comes to the gospel. Hell is never mentioned in the book of Acts, for instance, which records many gospel presentations of the early church leaders. Why? Because the early Jesus-followers knew this one simple truth: the gospel is more about running toward Some*one* rather than about running away from some*thing*.

---

1. This is where I currently hang my theological hat. I tell my atheist friends that at least we can agree on one spiritual reality, and that is the nature of their eternal future.

Perhaps one of the reasons that some Christians beat the dead horse of sin and hell is that they see our current culture as being in denial about the problem that is tearing us apart. Too many people have jumped on the cultural bandwagon of saying that we are all good, all light, all perfect just as we are. And this kind of denial-based, self-soothing propaganda simply cannot be supported by the daily events reported on the nightly news. Who can look at the world today and say we are doing perfectly fine and that we shouldn't change a thing?

Yes, in the beginning God made us perfect, like himself. But we have to keep reading. After a couple of chapters of perfection, we arrive at Genesis 3. Adam and Eve walked away from God's love, listened to the wrong voice, reached for the wrong tree, and ate the wrong fruit. In so doing, our ancestors welcomed sin into their lives, into our species, and into our world. And it has been passed on to us.

Someone might complain that reaping the negative consequences of the sin of Adam and Eve just isn't fair. Why should we pay for someone else's bad decisions? Why should I, in the twenty-first century, be held accountable for the actions of Adam and Eve so long ago? The answer is twofold: the cost of love, and corporate solidarity.

THE COST OF LOVE

We experience the consequence of Adam and Eve's sin because there is a cost to love. We were made by love for love, and since love is a choice, we were given the chance to choose love for ourselves. God could have created anyone, but he *chose* to create us. He *chose* to love us. Now the question becomes, will we choose him back?

Love requires choice to be love. Without choice, love is a façade. Say a zombie apocalypse happened, and you and one other person were the last remaining people on earth (well, living, breathing people, anyway). If the other person turned to you and said, "I love you. You're the only person for me," it would lack the beauty of someone saying those same words to you in a world with billions of other options.[2]

So God gave the first people choice. In essence, God told them, "You can love me, trust me, and work with me to take care of this planet and each other. Or you can walk away from my design for your lives, but there will be a high cost." Adam and Eve chose independence from God, and we have been making similar choices ever since.

Free choice carries with it the very real risk that people might use those choices to screw things up for others. Adam and Eve did exactly that. They screwed things up for the rest of us. Ever since, all humans have been born with sin as a part of their spiritual makeup (Psalm 51:5).

But don't be too hard on Adam and Eve. There is no evidence that you would have done any better. Look at your own life, and mine—we are screwing things up for ourselves and for others all the time. Examples of this abound, and if you're honest with yourself, you can think of many. For one, just look at the state of the planet we will be leaving for the next generation.

We are all victims of poor choices made by others, and we are all victimizers of others because of our own poor choices. The circle of life is the cycle of sin. We need something to break the cycle and take away our shame.

CORPORATE SOLIDARITY

I will never forget my first touchdown. I had joined our high school football team for a variety of reasons—I needed the exercise, I wanted to be popular, and I liked the jackets. I didn't understand how football worked, but I didn't really have to. Because I was a "husky" boy, as my coach called it, I played on the line—defensive and offensive, I was ready to block or tackle on a moment's notice. That's all I needed to know.

---

2. This is not to say that arranged marriages are without love. Rather, they have the opportunity to grow in love through the infinite number of choices made to invest in the relationship.

We were in the fourth quarter of one game, and the score was tied. Tension was high, since the opposing team had moved the ball within a few yards of our end zone and they had the ball. What happened next was like a slow-motion replay. Their quarterback fumbled the ball, and I was just steps away from the oblong pigskin, which was bouncing around in random directions like some sort of confused kangaroo. I moved toward it with the focus of a high school superhero about to save the day. Lo and behold, the ball bounced in my direction, and I scooped it up. I pivoted on one foot and sprang into a full-throttle run towards the end zone. I was running so fast I felt as if I traversed the entire length of the football field in a second. I could hear all my teammates screaming my name.

I crossed the line in a blaze of confidence and joy. I was standing in the end zone! While I stood there wondering what kind of dance I should spring into, the opposing team tackled me. Why on earth would they do *that*? As I slowly got up, jostled and incensed, it finally dawned on me.

I was standing in our own end zone. I had run the wrong way.

The horn sounded, and the game was over. I had scored my first and final touchdown (or "safety" for two points, to be specific). I was a hero, all right—for the opposing side.

I learned something very important that day. When one player scores a touchdown, the *team* scores a touchdown. That is corporate solidarity. When we are on the same team, one person's achievement or failure is everyone's achievement or failure. When a player scores a goal in hockey, the team gets the point. When a player makes a basket in basketball, the team gets two points. And when a husky boy from Scarborough, Ontario, gets confused in the fourth quarter and runs into his own end zone, the team loses the game.

When our corporate head, Adam, walked away from God's love and God's life, our whole species experienced the separation of sin.[3]

---

3. As mentioned in a note in chapter 3, "Adam" and "human" are both translations of the same Hebrew word, *ha'adam*, derived from the Hebrew word for "dirt." It

ADAM 2.0

The good news is that the principle of corporate solidarity makes the reverse also possible. That is, the righteousness of Jesus can have a positive effect on us as long as we align ourselves with this "second Adam" instead of the first.

The apostle Paul writes, "For the sin of this one man, Adam, caused death to rule over many. But even greater is God's wonderful grace and his gift of righteousness, for all who receive it will live in triumph over sin and death through this one man, Jesus Christ" (Romans 5:17 NLT). And again, "For since death came through a man, the resurrection of the dead comes also through a man. For as in Adam all die, so in Christ all will be made alive" (1 Corinthians 15:21-22).[4]

Jesus is Adam 2.0—a fresh start for humanity. Like Adam, Jesus faced the temptation of the serpent, but he made the better choice. Now we can all choose to align ourselves with Christ and enter into corporate solidarity with him. Our other option is to stay aligned, by default, with Adam.

Shifting our identity from Adam to Christ is what salvation is all about. When we are "in Christ," we are on #TeamJesus, and we experience the benefits of what Jesus has done on our behalf. Jesus saves us from judgment and from wrath, as we will now see.

SAVED FROM JUDGMENT

Jesus said, "Very truly I tell you, whoever hears my word and believes him who sent me has eternal life and will not be judged but has crossed over from death to life" (John 5:24). Let those words ring in your soul: "has eternal life" and "will not be judged"

---

literally means "earth creature," or "earthling." According to the Bible, Adam the earthling was the first human—the proto-human—within which we all find our identity until we find it in Jesus, the new Adam.

4. You may notice that Eve seems to have dropped out of the picture in this logic. This is not because she doesn't matter but because "Adam" is used as a short form for Adam and Eve. The Genesis story allows for this, since "Adam" refers to the original earthling out of which God also made Eve. Distilling Adam and Eve down to the singular "Adam" also allows for Adam and Jesus to be clearly contrasted as the start and the restart of humanity.

and "has crossed over from death to life." Jesus is saying when we trust in him we now gain something—eternal life—and we will miss out on something—judgment.

That is the power of forgiveness. Forgiveness doesn't pretend sin never happened, but it does, at least from God's perspective, remove the consequences of what happened. When one person forgives another, the door is open to reconciliation. When a bank forgives a debt, the debt is removed. When a governing official forgives a prisoner, the prisoner is set free. And when separated family members forgive past hurts, the way is made clear for reunion.

In the Bible, this relationship-altering forgiveness is called being *justified*. "For all have sinned and fall short of the glory of God, and all are justified freely by his grace through the redemption that came by Christ Jesus" (Romans 3:23-24). Justification is a legal term meaning to be declared not guilty. As a child, I learned that one way to remember what justification means is to say that being justified makes me "just-as-if-I'd" never sinned. This is completely true but still incomplete. Justification means being *declared* innocent, and it also means to be *made* innocent, to be made right with God. To be justified literally means to be made righteous—to be "righteous-ified" (a literal translation of the Greek word), which is to say, made right in our relationship with God.

Sometimes after friends argue, then reconcile, one of them might want to confirm that their relationship is back on track by asking, "Are we good?" Justification is God saying, "We're good."

When we turn to Christ for forgiveness of our sins, the judgment of those sins dissolves like sugar in water.[5] This is why the apostle Paul could proclaim confidently that "there is *now* no condemnation for those who are in Christ Jesus" (Romans 8:1-2).

---

5. I'm fascinated by how images and analogies communicate. You get the point of this one, even though it is, technically, completely inaccurate. Sugar dissolved in water may disappear, but it is still present. In fact, we intentionally put sugar in our tea and other drinks because we want its invisible but enhancing effects. The more I think about it, this is the worst analogy ever. But you still get the point. (And yes, sometimes I overthink my analogies.)

There it is: this complete freedom from judgment is offered to all of us *right now*. We can now live with the confidence that "since we *have been* justified through faith, we *have* peace with God through our Lord Jesus Christ, through whom we *have* gained access by faith into this grace in which we *now* stand" (Romans 5:1-2). This "peace with God" means our relationship with God is no longer blocked by sin or rebellion on our side or wrath or judgment on God's side. God doesn't stand over us like an angry judge, but stands with us like a comforting and encouraging friend.

Justification is like God reaching into our future, grabbing hold of our final judgment on judgment day, and clicking, dragging, and dropping it into our present while declaring us "not guilty." We are free. Free from wrath and free from worry. We are free to live and love and long for the future to arrive, because we have been—not will be, but *have been*—already justified.

SAVED FROM WRATH

We've already seen how Jesus saves us from death, which is spiritual separation from God, and justifies us here and now so we can live free from fear of judgment.

The Bible also speaks about the "wrath" of God as something Jesus removes: "Whoever believes in the Son has eternal life, but whoever rejects the Son will not see life, for God's wrath remains on them" (John 3:36). This word *wrath* is a translation of the Greek word for anger—the emotion most associated with judgment.

In Romans 5:9-10, Paul writes, "Since we have now been justified by his blood, how much more shall we be saved from God's wrath through him! For if, while we were God's enemies, we were reconciled to him through the death of his Son, how much more, having been reconciled, shall we be saved through his life!"

Saved from God's wrath. The original Greek literally says we are saved from "the" wrath instead of "God's" wrath, which paints a slightly different picture. Perhaps "wrath" is more like the natural consequences for our sin than the rage of an angry deity ready to hurl thunderbolts anytime we tick him off.

If a fish leaps out of the water and onto the dock, it will flop around for a while, but eventually it will die. It has left the environment for which it was made. Maybe God's wrath is like that: a sad consequence of our "I know better than God" choices to leave the environment of divine love we were meant to breathe. Some religious people paint a picture of God's wrath on judgment day that's more like an old man walking up and down a dock and beating all the naughty fish to death with his cane—or worse, wading through the water deciding which fish deserve to live and which fish deserve a beating and then throwing them up on the dock for eventual punishment.[6] But this isn't the picture of God's wrath we learn from the Bible.

Notice what Paul says about wrath near the beginning of Romans: "The wrath of God *is being* revealed from heaven against all the godlessness and wickedness of people, who suppress the truth by their wickedness" (Romans 1:18).

Paul says that God's wrath is already being revealed, already being experienced by people right now—all the time. What does that look like when it is expressed? The rest of the passage goes on to answer this question by repeating three times: "God gave them over" (vv. 24, 26, 28) to their own wills and their own ways. It seems as though God's wrath, then, refers to God simply letting us have what we demand. God's wrath means that eventually God gives us over to what we have chosen to stubbornly and destructively pursue, that God lets us go our own willful way. But it doesn't have to end that way. Right now, through Jesus, God is calling us back to himself.

I can't emphasize this strongly enough: *God is not angry with you.* He wants you to come home—not so you can receive some punishment he has waiting for you, but so you can escape the

---

6. I first heard this analogy used in a discussion with Joshua Ryan Butler. To be fair, this kind of theology is better represented by a man walking up and down a dock filled with "beached" fish and deciding which fish to throw back into the water and which fish to leave on the dock to die. But in the end, I'm not sure that clearing up that technicality helps get us closer to the God revealed through Jesus.

punishment you are already inflicting on yourself by creating distance between you and the love of God.[7]

BLOOD TRANSFUSION

If sin is an infection of our spiritual blood, then every generation passes it on. The situation seems dire, but the solution is effective and available for all.

The apostle John says, "The blood of Jesus . . . purifies us from all sin" (1 John 1:7). Yes, our blood is unclean. But the blood of Jesus is the blood of God—perfectly clean. And through Jesus, God offers us a kind of blood transfusion. The blood of Christ— that is, his life and his perfection—is offered to each of us as a way to be made whole.

Why was the death of Jesus so bloody? Why the brutality of crucifixion, and not hanging or lethal injection? The earthly answer is that crucifixion was the normal form of capital punishment used by the Romans in occupied countries in Jesus' time. The heavenly answer, however, is more interesting. The crucifixion of Christ not only shows us God's love but also demonstrates that Jesus shed his blood for our sin to cleanse us with his perfection. In the writings of the ancient Hebrews, blood is a powerful symbol of the total life of a person (see Genesis 4:10; Leviticus 17:11). So the bloody nature of Christ's death is saying something about the life-giving solution God offers our sin-sick souls.

I don't like images of crucifixion, whether portrayed in movies, paintings, or sculptures. Crucifixion is, after all, a form of inhumane torture to the point of death. But when I think about the cross of Christ, I look beyond all the blood to the life and healing and wholeness and reconciliation that the blood brings. That blood is the physical reminder of a spiritual reality that is good news for humankind.

---

7. Jesus' parable of the prodigal son (Luke 15) illustrates this idea of wrath. In that story, the closest thing we see to the wrath of the father is the pig farm where the son ends up after making a series of selfish choices. The father doesn't send the son there, but he does let the son experience the consequences of his own persistent choices. See chapter 12 for more on this.

And the good news keeps getting better.

When Jesus saves us—when his life overcomes our death and when his blood flows through our spiritual veins—we are healed *for good*. Our spirits are filled with the life of Christ, and all our sins are completely taken away (John 1:29), never to return.

That's right: we are healed, and *it stays that way*. All our sins, past, present, *and future*, are already gone and forgotten: "For I will forgive their wickedness and will remember their sins no more" (Hebrews 8:12).

Think of it this way: When Jesus died on the cross for our sins, how many of our sins were in the future? All of them! So you are not just cleansed and healed from your past sins; you are cleansed and healed from your future sins as well. You are now, and forever will be, right with God. Now we can go and live like it.

In the words of the apostle Paul in Ephesians 2:13, "But now in Christ Jesus you who once were far away have been brought near by the blood of Christ." That's reunion!

GOODBYE, GARBAGE

What are you carrying around from your past? What guilt or garbage haunts you? What experience from your past or habit in the present brings you shame when you think about it? For some of us, suppression, repression, and denial are the only ways we can cope with another day.

When we ignore our own sin, we're like people who store their garbage in the basement. Sure, "out of sight, out of mind" works for a while, but over time the pile builds up, and so does the smell. We can try to live as though it doesn't exist, and eventually we may even become used to the rotting smell. But sooner or later someone will notice what we don't, and our garbage will become known.

Some of us live with ongoing fear of the day that others discover our garbage. So we decorate our homes with air fresheners and never allow anyone to get too close. We keep busy. We do good deeds. We show keen interest in other people's lives, mostly to keep the spotlight off our own.

But there is a better way to live.

Jesus wants your garbage. He wants to take your trash away for good. He's willing and ready to take it to the dump for you. For free. He's the ultimate sanitation engineer.

Of course, there is something we need to do before the garbage collector can carry away all our rubbish: we need to take it to the curb. We need to stop hiding it and admit that we have garbage. And when we do, it will be gone for good.

The apostle John talked about the part we play in this process of spiritual housecleaning: "If we claim to be without sin, we deceive ourselves and the truth is not in us. If we confess our sins, he is faithful and just and will forgive us our sins and purify us from all unrighteousness" (1 John 1:8-9).

We need to admit, to acknowledge, our sin to Jesus. Then, and only then, can he clean things up. Taking our garbage out of the basement of denial to the curb of confession is how we become clean. How can God forgive our sin if we pretend we don't have any?

An essential part of this garbage removal is private confession between ourselves and God. But God ultimately intends for us to live in community where we can be "priests" to one another (Exodus 19:6; 1 Peter 2:9; Revelation 1:6). When we "come clean" and confess our sins to a trusted Christian brother or sister, he or she has an opportunity to remind us of God's grace in person. That can be powerful. That person's acceptance and embrace become the tangible expression of God's acceptance and embrace. And for some of us, this is the missing link to letting the healing message of God's full forgiveness settle in.

James, the half-brother of Jesus, encouraged Christians to "confess your sins to each other and pray for each other so that you may be healed" (James 5:16). As fellow sinners saved by grace, we can represent the nonjudgmental acceptance of God to one another when we have honest conversations about our failures and about God's embrace.

When we bring our garbage to one another, we confess and we pray and that's it. We don't condemn, we don't judge, we don't shame, and we don't give advice unless we are asked for it. We simply support each other in real relationships that are relationally "naked and unashamed." This is one way we live out the good news. And God uses it for our healing.

JESUS REUNITES

When Jesus met people, sometimes the first words out of his mouth were "Your sins are forgiven" (Matthew 9:2)—even before they had a chance to say hello! Obviously, Jesus was eager to get his point across: God is offering everyone forgiveness, a clean slate, and the chance to start again in reunited relationship, no matter what you've done or how far you've strayed.

So Jesus undoes the separation that sin has caused. He pulls the very separation that is sin into his own body on the cross and drags it down into death once and for all (this is the theme of Ephesians 2). And when he rises again, the sin stays dead and buried.

If sin separates, then:

Jesus *reunites*.

Jesus reunites *us*.

Jesus reunites us *with who we were*.

Jesus reunites us with who we were *meant to be*.

Jesus reunites us with who we were meant to be *with*.

Jesus reunites us with who we were meant to be with *forever*.

This has all been accomplished by Jesus. All that is left for us to do is simply accept that it is true, and then go live like it. That's what Jesus calls "faith."

ISN'T THIS MESSAGE DANGEROUS?

If you have been tracking with the extremely radical, sin-dissolving, wrath-removing, slate-cleaning, reuniting forgiveness that Jesus announces, then it might raise this question: Isn't this message dangerous? Couldn't people hear what they want to hear—that any sin they have ever done and will ever do has already been forgiven by God? Couldn't someone abuse this message to support committing more sin and living an even worse life?

If you're asking this question, then that's a good sign. It means that you're getting a glimpse of the really radical nature of the gospel. The answer to the question of whether the good news Jesus preached—of God's front-end-loaded salvation, forgiveness, and reconciliation—can be abused is . . . *yes*! The gospel is a risky message. But most things that will change the world are risky, and this is the biggest world changer of them all.

The gospel is rooted in the assumption that radical and risky grace, when properly understood and fully embraced, will inspire the best in us. God is betting on this one hope: that when you and I stare into the message of his unconditional love, his infinite grace, and his life-renewing forgiveness, we will experience a shift in our desires and values. God believes that grace will inspire us to live better lives, not use it as an excuse to live worse ones. And he offers the indwelling of his Holy Spirit to help this happen (Acts 2:38).

The apostle Paul writes that *grace*—not more rules or threats of punishment, but the grace that comes to us through Christ—"teaches us to say 'No' to ungodliness and worldly passions, and to live self-controlled, upright and godly lives" (Titus 2:12). When someone's love has changed your life for the better, when someone has loved you in transforming ways, when someone has loved you beyond what you deserve, don't you want to let your life be one of gratitude? Really, gratitude is the only appropriate response to grace.

SO MUCH MORE

For many Christians, what we have studied so far about the gospel—God's love and salvation from sin—forms the entirety of their gospel emphasis. Remember our review of popular four-point gospel summaries in chapter 6? Most of them go something like this: because God loves us, he sent Jesus to die on the cross to save us, and now all we have to do is respond by faith and receive this gift of salvation.

That *is* really good news. But frankly, it's just a fraction of the gospel.

Yes, through Jesus we are saved: from sin, from wrath, from hell, from judgment. But God not only saves us *from* something; he saves us *to* something and Some*one*. And that is what the rest of this book is about.

Are you ready? The best is yet to come.

9
OFF THE MAP

The gospel is less about how to get into the Kingdom of Heaven after you die, and more about how to live in the Kingdom of Heaven before you die.

—DALLAS WILLARD

JESUS IS GOD WITH US, COME TO

SHOW US GOD'S LOVE,   SAVE US FROM SIN,   **SET UP GOD'S KINGDOM, AND**   SHUT DOWN RELIGION,

SO WE CAN SHARE IN GOD'S LIFE.

Playing Risk, a board game based on a map of the world, is one of the fastest ways to start a family argument. Each player tries to set up a kingdom and establish total global domination by taking over other countries. Nations, provinces, and territories are reduced to spaces on a map that are clearly defined by lines that represent their borders. Each player can easily point to a place on the map and say, "I want to invade the country of so-and-so," or "It looks like Bob has control of the kingdom of such and such, and I want it. Time to attack!" (Sorry, Bob.)

In the real world, however, a country is much more than lines on a map or a plot of land. A country is also a way of living. Every nation has its own culture, history and heritage, language or languages, style of government, economy, and foreign policy, each defining the kind of influence that country has on the other countries. So the kingdoms of this world are *more than* places on a map, but they *are* on a map. They are physical, geographical, identifiable realities.

So where is the kingdom of Christ in all this?

Off the map.

Sort of.

JESUS NATION

The idea of a kingdom was an important concept for Jesus. He often said things like, "The kingdom of God has come near. Repent and believe the good news!" (Mark 1:15). For Jesus, the "good news" had something to do with the coming of "the kingdom of God." In fact, the Bible summarizes the entire message of Jesus as "the good news of the kingdom" (Matthew 4:23; Luke 4:43; Acts 8:12; 28:31).

According to Jesus, this kingdom is not a physical place or plot of land, although we live it out locally in the physical world. The kingdom of God is *a way of living* with Jesus our king; a way of being a part of what he is doing in the world, no matter where we live.

The word *kingdom* isn't used frequently anymore. Today we talk about nations and countries more than kingdoms. But *kingdom* (Greek: *basileia*) still has value when talking about the gospel, because it includes the word *king* (*basileus*): the one who shapes the vision and values of the *king*dom.

For Jesus, the word *kingdom* refers to a realm of relationship with God and others that is in harmony with God's will and God's way. This kingdom living isn't always easy, but it is the most satisfying way to be in this world, because it resonates with who and how we were made to be.

The kingdom of Christ is not contained by any earthly border, but it has representatives embedded within earthly kingdoms. These representatives may be citizens of the country in which they are physically living. But citizens of Christ's kingdom are less *citizens of* the land in which they live than they are *ambassadors to* the people of that land.

My passport says I am a Canadian citizen. I was born in Canada, grew up in Canada, and have always lived in Canada. I like being Canadian. I appreciate our prime minister, I enjoy our culture, and I celebrate our diversity. But in my heart, mind, priorities, and practices, my primary identity is *Christian*, not *Canadian*. I am more of an ambassador *to* Canadians than I am a Canadian. In fact, I have been commissioned by my true King to represent his kingdom to the people of Canada—and beyond when possible.

Our church, The Meeting House, like any church, is a little embassy in a foreign land, where the culture of the kingdom of Christ can be cultivated and experienced by anyone who visits. Every follower of Christ is part of a growing movement of people who refuse to let the kingdoms of this world—political, religious, ethnic, and economic kingdoms—diminish the love they live out toward one another.

We said before that Jesus doesn't just offer to save us *from* something, but *to* something. One way of identifying that something is "the kingdom of God." This good news of the kingdom is one of the most exciting yet neglected dimensions of the gospel. Recall our review of common four-point summaries of the gospel in chapter 6. Most of them stop before they get to this life-altering good news. And that's a tragic loss, because the kingdom is a holistic concept that keeps the gospel engaged in this world (rather than just make people wish for the next world). The kingdom to which we belong will shape our

- loyalty (to our king and country);
- laws (how we discern right and wrong); and
- lifestyle (cultural norms).

INSIDE OUT

When explaining the good news of the kingdom to religious people
in his day, Jesus often had to distinguish between his kingdom and
the kind of kingdom that people were expecting. Many assumed that
God's kingdom on earth would be a physical kingdom established
by force. They believed that when the Messiah came, he would be a
kind of warrior king who would make it all happen. Religious people often want God to bring about an earthly, religio-political kingdom by any means necessary, much like Israel during Old Testament
times, or Rome during New Testament times, or as some religious
terror organizations are trying to establish today. In democracies
like the United States, this often takes the more modest shape of religious people talking about the United States as a "Christian nation"
and praying and politicking to get the "right" candidate in office so
they can "get this nation back to God." But this kind of thinking
betrays a faulty understanding of the kind of kingdom God wants.

In one conversation about his kingdom with the religious leaders of his day, Jesus explained the distinction this way: "The coming of the kingdom of God is not something that can be observed,
nor will people say, 'Here it is,' or 'There it is,' because the kingdom of God is in your midst" (Luke 17:20-21). These words of
Jesus contain two important attributes of the kingdom of God.

First, the kingdom of God is not *something that can be
observed*—a visible structure or geographical location. We don't
establish the kingdom of God in a specific place with architecture
and armies, politics and power plays. It's not a religious organization or political party. This kingdom goes deeper than that.

Second, the kingdom of God is *in your midst*. The original
Greek for that sentence literally says the kingdom of God is
"within" you, from a Greek word that means "inside." At the
same time, the "you" is plural, the way some people might say
"y'all" or "all y'all."

So Jesus seems to be saying that the kingdom of Christ is a way
of living that: (a) exists within the hearts of individuals; and (b) is
expressed through the relationships between those individuals. An

accurate rendition of this verse would read, "The kingdom of God is inside you all together." After all, a kingdom is made up of individual citizens, but it is never a solitary experience. It is always personal, but it is never private.

CLOSER THAN YOU THINK

Jesus proclaimed that "the kingdom of God has come near" (Mark 1:15). The Greek for that sentence literally says the kingdom of God is "at hand." In other words, Jesus brings God's kingdom so close you can reach out and touch it, grab hold of it, and enter it. The good news of the kingdom is that we can participate in God's will and God's way on earth as it is in heaven.

Expressing the gospel in terms of the kingdom reminds us that Jesus' message isn't primarily about how to go to heaven when we die, but about heaven coming to earth while we live. This is what Jesus taught his followers to pray for: "Thy kingdom come, Thy will be done in earth, as it is in heaven" (Matthew 6:10 KJV).

As Jesus uses it, *kingdom* is a relational word. It orients our relationships in terms of a king, other subjects within the kingdom, and other kingdoms. Being an active part of the kingdom of Christ will influence how we relate to other kingdoms, such as the country in which we live and the kingdoms of culture, politics, business, media, and more. Being a citizen of Christ's kingdom will mean standing opposed to any ideas, attitudes, influences, emotions, or spiritual forces that are antihuman and anti-God.

If we embrace Jesus as our king, then the kingdom of heaven is within us. But it is not meant to stay there. We are meant to live out the reality of the kingdom in our lives, our relationships, and our priorities.

NOT OF THIS WORLD

When Jesus was arrested and stood before the Roman governor Pontius Pilate, the conversation naturally turned to the issue of kingdom. Was Jesus really claiming to be a king of a new kingdom? If so, he was a potential threat to Roman rule.

Pilate wanted to know where he stood with this guy, so he cut right to the chase and asked Jesus if he was the king of the Jews. Jesus replied, "My kingdom is not of this world. If it were, my servants would fight to prevent my arrest by the Jewish leaders. But now my kingdom is from another place" (John 18:36).

Not of this world? Some take this to mean that the kingdom of Jesus is something we should look forward to experiencing after we die. They see kingdom as a kind of synonym for heaven. Indeed, according to Matthew's gospel, Jesus regularly referred to his kingdom as "the kingdom of heaven" (e.g., Matthew 4:17; 10:7; 18:3; and more than twenty other instances).

But "heaven" was also a Jewish way of referring indirectly to God, as when someone says "Heaven help us," or "Thank heavens." Jews would often speak about God indirectly as a sign of respect, and Matthew's gospel was clearly written with a Jewish audience in mind. When we compare the same teachings in Matthew with the other gospels, we see that in the other gospels Jesus spoke about the "kingdom of God" (e.g., Mark 1:15; 10:14-15; Luke 4:43; 8:1; 16:16; 17:20-21; and more than thirty other references). That's what Matthew was referring to when he politely wrote "kingdom of heaven" for his Jewish readers. The kingdom of Christ, as Christ-followers would later refer to it (e.g., 2 Peter 1:11), is clearly the kingdom of a Person more than a place.

So back to our question: What was Jesus saying when he told Pilate that his kingdom is "not of this world"? The answer hangs on the meaning of the preposition *of*.

By saying that his kingdom is not "of" this world, Jesus was not saying that his kingdom is not *in* this world. Jesus had already taught that his kingdom is very much alive and active in this world. By saying that his kingdom is not "of" this world, Jesus was now clarifying, "My kingdom is not *from* this world, and not *produced by* this world." The kingdom of Christ is *in* this world, here and now, but this world has not produced it. It is *in* the world but not *of* the world. Christ's kingdom is different, in ethos and in attitude. It is a kingdom dedicated not to self-preservation and prosperity but to other-centered love, peace, and reconciliation.

When Pontius Pilate pushed Jesus to explain the nature of his kingdom, the one defining characteristic Jesus listed that made his kingdom different from all other kingdoms in this world was his followers' refusal to be violent. As Jesus put it, "My kingdom is not of this world. If it were, my servants would fight" (John 18:36).

Since the days of Constantine (272–337 CE), the first Roman emperor to embrace Christianity, the way of peace as a central characteristic of Christ's kingdom has too often been muted, if not completely forgotten. Emperor Constantine brought an end to the persecution of Christians and opened the way for Christianity to eventually become the official religion of Rome. Imagine! The very empire that was responsible for crucifying Christ now came to embrace the Christian religion! This must have seemed like a blessing from God at that time, but this wedding of church and state ended up betraying the gospel, with a kiss. The state lavished the church with riches, resources, protection, and power. And in return the church lavished the state with a convincing theology to support its violent rule and many wars. While we cannot judge Constantine's heart, we can say that the net effect of his post-conversion politics was disastrous for the cause of the gospel. Today, the Christian church is still fighting to purge these toxins from the body of Christ.

KINGDOM VERSUS CALIPHATE

"We've got to protect our borders." A man named Hank approached me after a talk about Jesus' way of peace that I gave at a church in the United States, and this is how he started a conversation.

"Tell me more," I invited.

"We're called by God to protect our own," he said. Okay, I thought to myself; this is going to be interesting.

"You're a Christian, yes?" I asked him. I wanted to confirm where he was coming from.

"Absolutely!" Hank confirmed. "Born and bred."

"Wonderful," I said. "Can you tell me more about where you got that idea? The idea that our first calling as Christians is to protect ourselves?"

And off he went on a five-minute, wandering rant. In it he covered these ten points:

1. We (the United States—he wasn't sure about Canada) are a Christian nation.
2. As a Christian nation, we need to defend the freedom and liberty God has given us.
3. Since God established this nation, it would be wrong to let it depart from the basics of the Bible.
4. The Bible says that the government bears the sword to execute God's judgement.
5. In the Old Testament, God called Israel to go to war many times to defend their land.
6. In the New Testament, Jesus said he came to bring a sword.
7. In the book of Revelation, Jesus comes back with a sword and he is covered in blood, ready to kick ass.
8. The Second Amendment of the U.S. Constitution says it is our right and responsibility as good citizens to bear arms.
9. Yes, Jesus might have said we should "turn the other cheek." But we've only got two cheeks, so eventually we should hit back. (I thought that one was clever.)
10. Therefore, good Christians should not be sissies and shrink from their responsibility to bear arms, protect our own, and defeat our enemies.

When Hank finished his rant, I could see he was convinced that he had just said some very convincing, very *Christian* things.

I began my response by saying, "Thank you, Hank, for sharing those thoughts. But it seems to me like you would make a better Muslim than a Christian."

Now I had his attention.

We had time, so one by one I began to respond to his arguments. My response went something like this:

1. There is no such thing as a "Christian nation," only Christian *people*—people of all nations who are part of the transnational, multiethnic kingdom of Christ.

2. The only kingdom that God has given us to defend is the kingdom of Christ, and we defend and advance this kingdom by confronting lies with truth and hate with love.

3. Christ-followers don't just follow "the basics of the Bible"; we follow Jesus. Besides, the United States was born out of rebellion against their rightful ruler in England at that time, even if he wasn't a very good one. It involved the manipulative and often violent acquisition of land filled with indigenous people—the Native Americans who were, well, here first. There is nothing particularly Christian about that beginning.

4. Yes, Romans 13 says Christians should support, pay taxes, and pray for the government who bears the sword—right after Romans 12, where it says that Christians themselves should not directly participate in the sword-bearing itself. The means and the ends of the state (Romans 13) are different from the means and ends of the church (Romans 12).

5. America is not Israel, and Jesus brought the new covenant and his new kingdom, which makes the old covenant obsolete (Hebrews 8:13).

6. The "sword" Jesus brought is not held by his followers. The message of Jesus might bring the sword, but the context to this teaching tells us that Jesus means *persecution of* Christians, not *violence done by* Christians. In fact, one disciple, Peter, made the same mistake and thought that Jesus meant he should carry a literal sword and not be afraid to use it. Jesus had to rebuke him for his error.[1]

---

1. This is one of three possible explanations on sword passages in the New Testament. The other two are (1) Jesus wanted his followers to become violent; and (2) the sword his followers should use is a metaphor for the message of the gospel. It is

7. The "sword" that Jesus bears in the book of Revelation is coming out of his mouth—it is clearly his message. (Have you ever seen someone try to win a literal sword fight while holding a sword in the mouth? I haven't either. Because that would be stupid.) And Jesus is said to be covered in blood before the battle even begins. This is his own blood shed for his enemies, not the blood of his enemies shed at his hand.

8. Christ-followers are ultimately citizens of a different kingdom and a different *kind* of kingdom. We are ambassadors to our earthly nation on behalf of Christ's country, where nonviolence is the norm. There is no Second Amendment in the Jesus Nation. The only way we "bear arms" is by wearing T-shirts.

9. How many times did Jesus say we should forgive? Seventy times seven. That's a lot of cheek.

10. The Bible says good Christians should not shrink back from laying down their lives while loving their enemies. It is always Christlike to die for a cause, just never to kill for a cause.

I then explained to Hank that his misunderstandings of the way of Christ were more rooted in the example of Muhammad than Jesus. If we can believe the traditions of Muhammad's life (the hadiths), Muhammad fought dozens of battles to establish and then defend an earthly, religiopolitical kingdom called a caliphate. The caliphate is a physical kingdom where the law of the land (sharia law) and the religion of the land (Islam) are fused together as a single way of life. In the caliphate, there is no separation between religion and politics, between church and state. When it comes to understanding

certainly used this way in the writings of the early church leaders (see, e.g., Ephesians 6:17; Hebrews 4:12). The third explanation, as outlined in the text, is that while the "sword" may be literal, it is used *against* his followers and not *by* them. I followed this third explanation for the specific passage Hank had in mind, but the second is also applicable for other passages. What we can rule out with a high degree of confidence is the first option. We simply have no written record of any church leader during the first three centuries of the movement (before Constantine) interpreting Jesus as encouraging violence under any circumstances.

"the kingdom of God," Muhammad and Jesus offer very different visions. I expect my Muslim friends to align with Muhammad. I expect people who call themselves Christians to align with Christ.

SHARIA LOVE

Recall that every kingdom shapes, and is shaped by, its loyalty, laws, and lifestyle. The kingdom of Christ is a way of living loyal to Jesus, but what kind of law governs the actions of its citizens?

In Christ's kingdom, the law of the land can be boiled down to one value that fulfills all laws: love. Love is our *sharia*, an Arabic word meaning "way" or "path."

Love trumps law as the guiding principle of Jesus. Law is case specific, whereas love is universally applicable. Law is shaped by culture, whereas love shapes cultures by shaping hearts. In fact, when love leads our hearts, rules become redundant.

This kind of teaching didn't go over very well with some of the religious elite in Jesus' day. And today, little has changed. Religious people, including and especially the most dedicated, like rules. Expected and even mandated patterns of behavior are easy because they are clear. "Just tell us what to do and we'll do it" is the cry of many religious people who value clarity over caring.

On one occasion, Jesus was approached by a religious leader with a most important question: "Teacher, which is the greatest commandment in the Law?" the leader asked.

Jesus replied: "'Love the Lord your God with all your heart and with all your soul and with all your mind.' This is the first and greatest commandment. And the second is like it: 'Love your neighbor as yourself.' All the Law and the Prophets hang on these two commandments" (Matthew 22:36-40).

Love God with all you've got, and love your neighbor as yourself. That's the whole kit and caboodle, according to Jesus. On the surface his answer is incredibly simple. But if we look beneath the surface, we'll see that it is also incredibly profound.

Do you see what Jesus did there? Jesus wasn't asked for the top two commandments. He was asked for *the* greatest commandment.

But in his response, Jesus showed that he wouldn't let us separate love for God from love for one another. He knew that just loving God with all our heart, soul, mind, and strength without an equal commitment to love our neighbor as we love ourselves could lead to expressions of religious piety that ignore the hurting people around us, or worse, actually hurt people around us. People blow themselves and others up for "love of God." Other people dedicate their lives to meditating in monasteries while ignoring the hurting world around them for "love of God." So Jesus tied our love for God together with our love for others. In fact, this bidirectional spirituality of Jesus teaches us that the *primary* way we love God is through loving others (see Matthew 25:31-46).

Near the end of his life, Jesus so much wanted to emphasize to his disciples the need to fuse their love for God together with practical, caring, other-centered love for one another that he skipped right over the first command and summed everything up in just the second: "A new command I give you: Love one another. As I have loved you, so you must love one another. By this everyone will know that you are my disciples, if you love one another" (John 13:34-35).

Two things changed from Jesus' earlier statement of bidirectional love: First, Jesus placed what appears to be exclusive emphasis on what was the second commandment to love one another. Second, Jesus had altered the second commandment (now the one central command). Jesus told his followers not just to love others as they love themselves, but to love them the way he—*Jesus*—loved them. That is a big love upgrade.

The early church embraced this new moral code and adopted the "love others above all" ethic as the sum total of the law of the land in the kingdom of Christ (e.g., Romans 13:8; Galatians 5:14; Ephesians 5:2; James 2:8; 1 Peter 4:8; 1 John 3:14-18; 4:19-21).

Many religions have pious practices designed to please God: lengthy pilgrimages to holy shrines; daily prayers at specific times; holy ceremonies in holy buildings led by holy men wearing holy clothes while they perform holy rituals. But for Christ-followers,

simply loving others as Jesus does is our highest form of worship
and the central ceremony of our religion (James 1:26-27).

THE LIFESTYLE OF PEACE

At our church, The Meeting House, I am blown away by the diversity of people who call each other brother and sister and who relate
to one another as valuable family members. I'm talking about people not just of different races, ages, styles, and stages of life, but
also of different personality types, levels of education, occupations,
orientations, and religious backgrounds. And we all do life together
as one large extended family, sometimes all together and most often
in small, family-style house groups called "home churches."

There's nothing quite like "church." A place where very different kinds of people who have nothing but Jesus in common gather
together to learn how to live a loving life with one another.

God's kingdom is a kingdom of peace, in which the borders
that separated humankind into subgroups of nationality, race, and
culture are rendered meaningless. Now we are all citizens of a new
nation that crosses all national boundaries. We are members of
a new race that includes all races. And we are residents of a new
country that has its own culture of inclusion and embrace.

When God reigns in our lives, peace is the result. The Hebrew
word for peace is *shalom*, and it refers to more than an inner calm.
Shalom is peace plus justice. It is a peace *within* ourselves, but also
peace *between* ourselves and others.

Jesus grants us a peace within ourselves that transcends circumstances (John 16:33; Philippians 4:7), as well as peace in our relationships with others we might otherwise avoid. The early church
announced the gospel as "the good news of peace through Jesus
Christ, who is Lord of all" (Acts 10:36; see also Ephesians 6:15).

One of the greatest sociological divides in human history
has been the division between Jews and Gentiles (non-Jews). At
the time of Christ, this division was at its zenith. Romans had
invaded Israel, and Jews had to live surrounded by their Gentile
oppressors. This was especially hard for Jews who believed that,

as God's "chosen people" living in the Promised Land, they should be allowed to live in peace, all by themselves.

But the early Christians were convinced that Jesus, the Jewish Messiah, had made a way for Jews and Gentiles to be one family together. He did this by tearing down the wall of the old covenant religion, which was predicated on separation through rules and rituals. If this were true—if Jesus really accomplished this—it would be the greatest sociological miracle of all time.

The apostle Paul wrote about this countercultural truth when describing what Jesus accomplished through his crucifixion:

> For he himself is our peace, who has made the two groups one and has destroyed the barrier, the dividing wall of hostility, by setting aside in his flesh the law with its commands and regulations. His purpose was to create in himself one new humanity out of the two, thus making peace, and in one body to reconcile both of them to God through the cross, by which he put to death their hostility. He came and preached peace to you who were far away and peace to those who were near. For through him we both have access to the Father by one Spirit.

> Consequently, you are no longer foreigners and strangers, but fellow citizens with God's people and also members of his household. (Ephesians 2:14-19; see also Colossians 1:20)

This was earth-shattering news at the time, and not everyone was pleased to hear it—particularly those who wanted to harbor hatred, retaliation, and prejudice.

And because Jesus has accomplished this peace on our behalf, those of us who are citizens of this new "kingdom of heaven" on earth practice peace as a way of life. For us, people are never the enemy, but victims of the enemy. People are in need of rescue, not retaliation. Jesus-followers should always be ready to *die* for a cause but never willing to *kill* for one.

THE STRATEGY OF ADVANCE

As in the board game Risk, real-life earthly kingdoms go to war to acquire land and the resources that come with that land. Kingdoms use force to acquire land and then use force or the threat of force to rule that land, as well as to defend it against other kingdoms that might want to take that land for themselves.

The kingdom of Christ also wants to advance, but the land we fight for is the space of separation between one another. That's the "land" that God wants us to acquire. Jesus-followers believe that reconciliation is at the heart of the gospel, and we will "fight" hard to help broken relationships, with God and with each other, come back together again.

This means that our kingdom warfare is not *against* other people but *for* other people. We fight against any power—political, societal, or spiritual—that divides rather than unites, or that promotes hate rather than love. And we do this in ways that treat people not as the enemy but as victims of the true enemy.

The apostle Paul wrote that "our struggle is not against flesh and blood, but against the rulers, against the authorities, against the powers of this dark world and against the spiritual forces of evil in the heavenly realms" (Ephesians 6:12).

Some people believe in a real, literal Satan, while other people think the devil is a metaphor for evil. Personally, because I believe that Love and Goodness are more than just detached concepts but are ultimately expressed in a real, literal, personal God who is Love, I have no problem believing that evil itself is more than a vague concept but is ultimately expressed through actual personhood. In the Bible, that locus of personal evil is known by many names, such as the serpent, Satan, the devil, or the evil one.

The really good news is that Satan is now defeated, through the upside-down power of love expressed through the cross of Christ. Jesus "disarmed the powers and authorities, he made a public spectacle of them, triumphing over them by the cross" (Colossians 2:15). Sure, the devil can attack us with the only weapon he has left—manipulation through deception—but his power lacks any real teeth. It is all smoke and mirrors, posturing in order to intimidate, confuse, and distract. Unfortunately, this approach works on us far too often.

"For though we live in the world, we do not wage war as the world does," the apostle Paul said. "The weapons we fight with are not the weapons of the world. On the contrary, they have divine power to demolish strongholds. We demolish arguments and every pretension that sets itself up against the knowledge of God, and we take captive every thought to make it obedient to Christ" (2 Corinthians 10:3-5).

Our fight is not against people but against ideas ("arguments and every pretension that sets itself up against the knowledge of God"). Some ideas are just bad ideas. These bad ideas are anti-love and anti-the-God-who-is-Love, and sometimes they become so popular that they are like strongholds. They are like military bases of bad ideas. So we are called to fight against these bad ideas with good, true, and loving ones. In fact, Paul used the metaphor of taking prisoners: we take those thoughts captive and turn them around so that they serve Jesus.

In the end, our motivation is clear: we love truth, we love God, and we love people too much to let them continue as P.O.W.s of bad ideas.

THE TACTIC OF ENEMY LOVE

As ambassadors for the kingdom of Christ, we love our enemies because that is the will of our king, the way of our culture, and the foreign policy of our government.

But what do we hope to accomplish through this radical action? What is the goal, the intended outcome?

Enemy love arrests a process of hate and aggression with a new element. If even for just a moment, active enemy love injects a foreign ingredient into a culture of violence, offering everyone who experiences it a moment of light and an opportunity to wake up to reality.

Reconciliation leading to reunion—God turning enemies into his friends and even family—is at the heart of the gospel. The apostle Paul wrote, "For if, while we were God's enemies, we were reconciled to him through the death of his Son, how much

more, having been reconciled, shall we be saved through his life!"
(Romans 5:10). The kingdom of Christ—God's will and way lived
out in our relationships—was founded by a King who loved his
enemies to the end. Why would the citizens of the kingdom live
any differently?

If reconciliation is the goal, then Christ-followers fight for that
goal by loving. Love is our only tactic. It may not always work
right away. We may suffer loss in the process, and in some extreme
cases we may even die trying. But as the gospel shows us, sometimes dying is what it takes to help someone else see the truth.

Jesus not only embodied this radical, nonviolent enemy love in
how he lived and how he died; he also taught it to his followers as
the only way to advance his kingdom.

> You have heard that it was said, "Eye for eye, and tooth for
> tooth." But I tell you, do not resist an evil person. If anyone
> slaps you on the right cheek, turn to them the other cheek also.
> And if anyone wants to sue you and take your shirt, hand over
> your coat as well. If anyone forces you to go one mile, go with
> them two miles. Give to the one who asks you, and do not turn
> away from the one who wants to borrow from you.
>
> You have heard that it was said, "Love your neighbor and hate
> your enemy." But I tell you, love your enemies and pray for
> those who persecute you, that you may be children of your
> Father in heaven. He causes his sun to rise on the evil and the
> good, and sends rain on the righteous and the unrighteous. If
> you love those who love you, what reward will you get? Are
> not even the tax collectors doing that? (Matthew 5:38-46)

This was radical teaching at the time, especially for those living
under a brutal, oppressive regime like that of the Romans. But it
helped launch a world-changing movement, and it is a truth that
is central to Christ's kingdom today.

When we actively turn the other cheek, we remind our attacker
of the facts: we are not a passive punching bag, but a person with
the power of choice—a power our attacker can never take away

from us. And when we go the second mile, we demonstrate that we are freer than our oppressors ever imagined.

THE SECOND MILE

Let's look more closely at the example of going the second mile. Jesus taught this against the backdrop of Roman oppression. To get a sense of context, imagine what it would be like if the Nazis had won World War II and were now the occupying force in your country. Or imagine if a radicalized Islamic movement were now in power, exerting dominance through regular, graphic public executions, high taxation, and ongoing insult. That is what it was like for Jews at the time of Jesus.

Israel was a conquered and oppressed nation, and Jewish people lived every day with a foreign military presence around them that reminded them of their powerless state. When Jesus said "Love your enemies," his audience didn't have to wonder who he was talking about. Jesus' Sermon on the Mount wasn't Theoretical Religious Philosophy 101. It was a real-world love ethic for a real-world hate context.

Romans soldiers were allowed to compel any conquered citizen to carry their gear for them for one mile. To prevent complete abuse of their power, Roman military law demanded that at the end of that mile, the soldier needed to release the citizen and choose another citizen for the next mile.

Imagine leaving your home one afternoon to run an errand, perhaps to go to the local market, and seeing a Roman soldier walking nearby. You'd probably walk in the opposite direction or just try really hard not to make eye contact. You'd hope he didn't call you, or you could be forced to carry his heavy gear for a full mile out of your way.

Now imagine you have been pressed into submission and forced to carry a soldier's gear. If you are a Christ-follower, then while you walk alongside your "enemy" under the burden of his weapons of war, you take the time to remind yourself and meditate on the reality of who this soldier *really* is. He is a man made in the image of God and infinitely precious to his Creator. This Roman's race, religion, and the role he plays as your oppressor fade into obscurity compared to the love you know God has for him. Here is a man who has been victimized since childhood by the lies of an oppressive state; a system that taught him wrong was right, that hate was justified, and that violence was godly. Yes, you are at war, but not with him. You are at war with the bad ideas that have put you both into this situation.

And so, at the end of the mile, when the Roman centurion releases you from your obligation and begins to look for another person to press into his service, you change the power dynamic through love. You don't drop his gear but instead offer to keep walking with him. At first he is confused. This experience is beyond his paradigm for understanding life. But not wanting to get into an argument with a person who is trying to be more helpful than he has a category for, the Roman accepts your offer and off you go again. Now everything has changed—for you and for him.

For you, *while the first mile was oppression, the second mile is freedom.* While the first mile was compulsion, the second mile is volition. While the first mile was an expression of systematic hate, the second mile is a revelation of reconciling love. While the first mile is the way of the kingdom of Rome, the second mile is the way of the kingdom of Christ.

For the soldier, while the first mile was another mindless business-as-usual activity, the second mile is a shock to his political, religious, and cultural systems. It forces everything into a humanizing relationship. For him, the choice you made was a moment of potential illumination. The second mile you walked has provided him a longer time of contemplation on the role he is playing. Now you have given him the opportunity to see life differently, to wake up from his slumber of role-playing power. You have given him the chance to see you as more than a slave, the chance to see you as a fellow human being. You have helped him to see himself as more than an oppressor, to see himself as one in need of a new paradigm for perceiving this world.

On the surface, enemy love may or may not "work" in any one situation. After all, Jesus loved his enemies and it got him killed. But followers of Jesus don't live life on the surface. We look beneath skin tone and clothing, attitudes and accents. We look past the hatred of others to see the love of God for everyone, and we look past immediate outcomes in specific situations to the greater goal of the advancement of the kingdom of Christ.

AND NOW FOR THE SCANDAL

So Jesus came to show us God's love, save us from sin, and set up his kingdom. If these three aspects of the gospel were all that Jesus preached, he may not have gotten himself killed so quickly.

If Jesus had merely proclaimed, "God loves you and has a wonderful plan for your life," the religious leaders could have responded, "We know! That's why God rescued us out of Egypt and gave us the Torah to guide us!"

If Jesus had merely proclaimed, "God wants to save you from your sin," the religious leaders could have responded, "We know! That's why when God rescued us out of Egypt and gave us the Torah he also commanded that we make regular animal sacrifices!"

If Jesus had merely proclaimed, "God wants to set up his kingdom here on earth," the religious leaders could have responded, "We know! That's why when God rescued us out of Egypt and gave us the Torah, he also led us through the wilderness, across the Jordan, and gave us the land of Israel!"

But there was a fourth gift in the gospel proclamation of Jesus. It, more than anything else, sparked a scandal that would make Jesus public enemy number one. It would lead the religious leaders of his day to call for his immediate execution. In essence, Jesus proclaimed, "God loves you, wants to forgive you for all your sin, and set up his kingdom here on earth—and you no longer need your religion to experience any of this!"

Now that is a message some people thought was so threatening that it was worth killing for. It is certainly a message that Jesus thought was worth dying for.

10

REQUIEM FOR RELIGION

There was no religion in Eden and there won't be
any in heaven; and in the meantime Jesus has died
and risen to persuade us to knock it all off right now.
—ROBERT FARRAR CAPON

JESUS IS GOD WITH US, COME TO

**SHOW US
GOD'S LOVE,**

**SAVE US
FROM SIN,**

**SET UP GOD'S
KINGDOM, AND**

**SHUT DOWN
RELIGION,**

SO WE CAN SHARE IN GOD'S LIFE.

We come now to what is one of the most fascinating aspects of the gospel, and indeed, of all world religious history: God's promise and plan to replace religion with himself.[1]

Think of it: a world religious leader (in this case, the Messiah of Judaism) who claims to be on a mission to shut down his own religion? This is unprecedented and unparalleled in the history of all world religions. Whether or not someone is a believer in Jesus,

---

1. For more on this aspect of the gospel, see my book *The End of Religion*.

this one fact of history makes Jesus the most interesting man in the world, ever.

But wait: If Jesus came to shut down religion, why did he end up *starting* one of the world's biggest religions instead? That's a bit of a miss, isn't it?

This is a great question, and one we will address in this chapter. But first, let's clarify terms.

WHAT IS RELIGION?

The word *religion* stems from the Latin word *religare*, a combination of *re* (to return, to repeat) and *ligare* (to tie, to bind). Our English word *ligament* also comes from *ligare*, as ligaments bind various parts of the human body.

So religion can mean a fastening of the self to something important; a kind of anchoring, restraining, or reconnecting. Positively understood, religion is like the string tethering a kite to someone's guiding hands. Used this way, some people describe their connection to Christ as their "religion." In a world of detachment and disjointedness, this kind of yoking of the self to the Eternal is good. If that's how you use the word *religion*, this chapter still has something important to say to you. You will just have to make one adjustment: every time you read the word *religion*, you'll need to substitute a phrase like "religious legalism" or "empty religion" or "systems of salvation" or "prioritizing forms and formulas over faith, hope, and love."

While some people use the word *religion* to refer to an intimate, heartfelt connection with God, Jesus used a different word for that. He called this kind of trusting relationship *faith*. (The New Testament word for "faith" is *pistis*, which doesn't mean believing in ideas without evidence, but rather trusting in a person. Faith, or trust, is the foundational element to any healthy relationship. See chapter 12 for more on this.)

Jesus is never recorded as using the word *religion*.[2] Rather, he called people to an intimate faith connection with God as our

---

2. The biblical word for "religion" is *threskeia*, a Greek word that refers to the outer rituals or practices associated with a belief. Like its Latin equivalent, *religare*,

Father and other Christ-followers as our brothers and sisters. *Jesus is more about relationship than religion.*

You see, there is also a negative meaning to this word *religion*. Remember, the word stems from the Latin *religare*, a combination of *re* (to return, to repeat) and *ligare* (to tie, to bind). Quite literally then, religion can mean "a return to bondage." And when we look at the track record of many of the world's religions, past and present, this negative interpretation seems more than accurate. This kind of religion tries to capture ideas like faith, spirituality, holiness, and sacredness within codependent systems of salvation. Religion, therefore, acts as a kind of mediator between people and Ultimate Reality; a systematic, structural, or institutional intermediary; a broker of salvation that adds one more layer between us and God. But the only intermediary we need is Jesus himself, who is God becoming one of us.

The apostle Paul wrote, "There is one God and one Mediator who can reconcile God and humanity—the man Christ Jesus" (1 Timothy 2:5 NLT). We are missing the gospel whenever we let any one institution or person substitute for Jesus as our only mediator. Religious people are always in danger of rewriting 1 Timothy 2:5 in their hearts to read "There is one God and one mediator between God and humanity, and that is [the Roman Catholic Church, or the Bible and the Watchtower Tract Society, or The Meeting House, or this teacher, or that preacher, etc., etc.]."

One solid test to see if we are relying on Jesus or on a cheap substitute to be our connection to God is to ask ourselves if we believe people need to be a part of *our* particular organization, institution, denomination, or spiritual group in order to be right with God. (This is one of my primary protests against the belief system of my Jehovah's Witness friends.) As I tell people at The Meeting House, we will serve our purpose as a healthy church if we are a meeting

---

threskeia can be positive or negative, depending on the substance and focus of the belief it expresses. Jesus put the emphasis on "faith" because it works from the inside out, while "religion" works from the outside in. Unfortunately, religion sometimes never penetrates the soul but simply remains an empty shell of ritual.

place for people to draw closer to God and each other. But the day I start preaching that people need The Meeting House specifically in order to be right with God, I need to be fired.

That kind of religion is less like the string that helps a kite fly and more like a chain that prevents a kite from ever taking off. In fact, it makes it irrelevant whether the kite owner is holding on to the other end. Religion doesn't need God at the other end—the system functions fine without him.

This is why, when someone asks me if I am religious, most of the time I answer something like, "Well, you might describe me that way. But I tend to think of myself as more spiritual than religious. Either way, one thing I can tell you is that I'm really into Jesus."[3]

For Jesus, religion was like a big fat finger pointing to God but obstructing everyone's view. So he had to shut it down. And the way he did this was absolutely ingenious.

So, what happens when the Divine comes to us directly? What are the implications for religion when Ultimate Reality enters our world (through Jesus) and enters us (through the Holy Spirit)? What does it mean to say that God, through Jesus, replaces religion with himself? Let's look at five aspects of religion—sacrifices, priests, temples, rituals, and rules—that God replaces.

REPLACING SACRIFICES

For us to live, something has to die: this concept of sacrifice is central to almost all ancient religions.

Sin was the great problem, and salvation was the great need. To get forgiveness, a person would need a priest to make a sacrifice on her or his behalf—a way of giving God or the gods a gift in order to obtain favor. This would restore balance to the Force.

This never-ending ritual of offering animal, human, or food sacrifices put the responsibility on humans to make the gods

---

3. This way of thinking about ourselves as "spiritual" people (Greek *pneumatikos*) is in keeping with how the New Testament authors spoke about themselves (e.g., 1 Corinthians 2:15; 3:1; Galatians 6:1; 1 Peter 2:5).

happy with us (or at least to stop being mad at us), to forgive us, to answer our prayers, and maybe even to pay attention to us. We needed to do the right ritual in order to make a basically angry deity change his mind and become kind toward us.

When Jesus first stepped onto the scene of public ministry, John the Baptist pointed at him and said, "Look, the Lamb of God, who takes away the sin of the world!" (John 1:29). That one subversive statement told everyone that the whole system was about to get a makeover. Let's look more closely.

First, "the Lamb of God." Lambs were what humans provided for religious sacrifices. But Jesus is the Lamb provided by God, not by us. Jesus is God's gift of grace—doing for us what we have been trying to achieve through religion.

Second, "who takes away." At the very moment John was saying this about Jesus, lambs and other animals were being slaughtered in the Jerusalem temple nearby, and other religious places around the world, in order to take away sin. But if Jesus takes away the sin of the world, then all those other sacrifices would instantly be rendered obsolete.

Third, "the sin of the world." Jesus takes away not just some sins (plural), but the sin (singular)—that is, the whole sin problem. And the sin that Jesus removes is the sin of the world—not just the sin of one group of people in one specific religious sect, at one specific point in time, but of everyone.

John was essentially saying, "Hey everybody! Forget about sacrificing another lamb, because Jesus will take away all sin for all people once and for all!" The gospel is God's good news that not only can we be saved from our sin but we also can be saved from our religion.

This message was a setup for an eventual confrontation with the brokers of religion. There were a lot of religious people who depended on that system for their salvation, and a lot of religious leaders who depended on that system for their livelihood. The sort of spirituality Jesus advocated puts religion out of a job, and there were many people in Jesus' day who felt he needed to be stopped and his message silenced.

Ironically, when the religious leaders of Jesus' day became so threatened by his end-of-sacrifice message that they called for his crucifixion, they were actually enabling Jesus to become the sacrifice he had intended to become. The irony of ironies is that the religious leaders facilitated the sacrifice that, once and for all, would make all other religious sacrifice redundant.

Now we are free from that bloody ritual, free to live as already-forgiven-and-loved-by-God people. Whenever we doubt that God really does love and forgive and accept us, we can look back at the cross of Christ as a vivid reminder that God himself provided the last sacrifice. There is no need to repeat what God has done once and for all. This is why the Bible speaks of God's forgiveness for his children as past tense, as over and done with (see Colossians 2:13-14; 1 John 2:12; Ephesians 4:32; Hebrews 10:17-18). When, on the cross, Jesus cried out, "It is finished" (John 19:30), it really was. Forgiveness is accomplished. Religion is over. This is why the apostle Paul could proclaim so confidently that "there is now no condemnation for those who are in Christ Jesus" (Romans 8:1).

Now we live on the other side of the last sacrifice. All has already been set right between us and God. And the only sacrifices we offer are our very selves, living together in love as one giant "living sacrifice" (Romans 12:1). Living sacrifice: what an oxymoronic spirituality! Talk about two words that don't belong together—like jumbo shrimp, slumber party, guest host, plastic glasses, and country music. We are, together, a living sacrifice. We no longer worship God by killing; we worship God by living.

REPLACING PRIESTS

In the religious systems of Jesus' day, in order to have a sacrifice, you needed a priest to offer the sacrifice on behalf of the people. The idea of a priest is unique in the arena of spiritual leaders. A priest is more than a pastor (which means a shepherd) or a minister (which means servant) or an elder (which means mature). A priest is a mediator: a person who goes to God on behalf of the people and comes to the people on behalf of God.

There were many priests in Jesus' day, but there was only one high priest—the head of all the priests who worked at the temple in Jerusalem. Jesus became more than just the last sacrifice; he also became the last high priest who offers the sacrifice. The implications for this are massive. You better be sitting down for this one.

Sitting down usually means you are resting. When you are seated, the weight is off and your legs can trust the strength of the chair to do the work for you. Keep this in mind as you read on.

For all those centuries while the priests of Israel's religion performed their duties, it was protocol that they *remained standing*. Under the old covenant, the priest stood before the altar day after day, offering the same animal sacrifices again and again. The posture of the priests sent the world a message: "This is not over, folks. You will always need more sacrifices to be made on your behalf. This is an ongoing salvation system. Get used to it."

But the sacrifice of Christ is different. Very different. "Unlike the other high priests, he does not need to offer sacrifices day after day, first for his own sins, and then for the sins of the people. He sacrificed for their sins once for all when he offered himself" (Hebrews 7:27).

The sacrifice Jesus offered was unlike any other religious sacrifice offered by any priest, anywhere, anytime. It was the sacrifice to end all sacrifices: once for all, never to be repeated. Why? Because Jesus didn't just offer a lamb or a goat. He offered himself. More than *human* sacrifice, this is *divine* sacrifice.

And when he was done, when it was all finished—catch this— he *sat down*. "But when this priest had offered for all time one sacrifice for sins, he sat down at the right hand of God" (Hebrews 10:12). This play with posture in the book of Hebrews is saying something critical. The priests of religion *stand*, day after day, sacrifice after sacrifice. Their job is never done. But Jesus offered himself as the last sacrifice, once and for all time, and then he *sat down* to say, "It is finished."

There is no need to worry about the next sacrifice, the next religious duty, or the next good deed you have to do in order to get on God's good side. It's all been done.

Do we need priests today? Well, yes—and no. We don't *need* priests, because we *are* priests. The apostle Peter says that all believers in Jesus are "a royal priesthood" (1 Peter 2:9).[4] That's right: if you're a Jesus-follower, you just got a job promotion!

This means that, while Jesus is forever our great High Priest, we are all priests along with him. In Western culture, we might be tempted to apply this gospel truth by saying, "That means I don't need anyone else! I'm my own priest!" But in Eastern culture, which is far less individualistic and far more communal, this idea of the priesthood of all believers would lead one to say, "I don't need a paid professional holy man, because I am surrounded by brothers and sisters who can pray for me and share God's truth with me. And I can be that for them!" Now we can confess our sins to one another and pray for each other so that we can be healed of our guilt, shame, and bitterness (see James 5:16). The idea of the priesthood of all God's people should drive us toward one another to receive more from God through one another.

As the apostle Peter goes on to say, "Each of you should use whatever gift you have received to serve others, as faithful stewards of God's grace in its various forms" (1 Peter 4:10). We are, each of us, "stewards of God's grace" to one another. We are the channels God uses to dispense his grace. We may not need a special holy class of professionals called "priests," but we do need community, spiritual family, and authentic friendship. That's how

---

4. This idea of everyone being a priest for one another was the original vision of God for his people (compare 1 Peter 2:9 and Revelation 1:6 with Exodus 19:6). In Exodus 20:18-21 and Deuteronomy 5:25-27, we read a cryptic story about how God first tried to reveal his Ten Commandments to everyone directly, but because of their fear, the people asked Moses to function as their representative to God and as God's representative to them.

God works. In other words, we may not need religion, but we do need relationship.

REPLACING TEMPLES

Are you catching a glimpse of what was going on when Jesus died? Jesus was fulfilling the entire religious system through his own crucifixion. At the point of his death, Jesus was playing three roles: (1) the lamb being sacrificed; (2) the priest offering the sacrifice; and even (3) the temple itself, where the sacrifices happen. Jesus was summing up in his body and action the complete sacrificial system of his day. Jesus was being and doing all that religion was trying to be and do.

Religion thrives on holy geography and sacred architecture. For Jesus to thoroughly shut down religion, he needed to help us reconfigure our religious ideas of *where* we can go to meet with God. He needed to redefine what constitutes holy places and holy spaces.

Within the religion of Jesus' day, the temple was a place where the sacred presence of God dwelt and could be experienced in a specific way. Yes, God was omnipresent, but people believed the spirit of God was manifest in the holy temple in a unique way.

Jesus taught people that *he*, not some temple in Jerusalem or anywhere else, is the meeting place with God. He introduced an irreligious idea shift that would change the world forever. The apostle John records a conversation that Jesus had with religious leaders one day while standing outside the temple. Jesus told them, "Destroy this temple, and I will raise it again in three days" (John 2:19). The religious leaders thought Jesus was making some wild statement about the magnificent temple in Jerusalem, but then John adds this explanation: "But the temple he had spoken of was his body" (John 2:21).

Catch that? Jesus was saying that *he*—not some building—is the sacred space we come to in order to meet with and experience God's Spirit. This changes everything. We don't need a special building, cathedral, temple, shrine, or sanctuary to meet with God.[5]

But how do we "come to Jesus" as our temple today when he hasn't been physically present on this planet for two thousand years?

Remember that a temple is the place where God's Spirit dwells in a unique way. Jesus claimed to be God's temple when he was physically present on earth, but then Jesus introduced one more irreligious idea shift: he promised that when he left, his followers would become like the body of Christ and share in the same experience—the indwelling of the Holy Spirit, God's personal presence (John 15:26; 16:12-15; 17:26; Acts 1:8).

Today we are used to hearing people say things like "My body is a temple." (Well, people with *my* kind of body don't say that very often, but you get the point.) This idea stems from the irreligious teaching of Jesus and was meant to promote more than healthy eating and regular selfies taken after sessions at the gym. In fact, the early Christ-followers went beyond merely thinking of individual persons as individual temples of God (as in 1 Corinthians 6:19) to a more relational concept of God's temple. The early church spoke of us *together* making up one organic, relational, and revolutionary "body of Christ" (1 Corinthians 12; Ephesians 4:15-16) that was in fact one unified temple of God (e.g., 1 Corinthians 3:16; 2 Corinthians 6:16; Ephesians 2:21-22).

Jesus himself had said, "For where two or three gather in my name, there am I with them" (Matthew 18:20). That's temple language. This doesn't mean that Jesus isn't with us when we are by ourselves, but that there is some deeper experience of his personal presence that we are meant to have when we come together.

---

5. At the time of Jesus, the idea of a biblical religion without a temple, priests, and sacrifices was far-fetched. Then, in the year 70 CE, the Romans quashed a Jewish rebellion and destroyed the Jerusalem temple. It has never been rebuilt and sacrifices have never resumed. Within one generation of Jesus, the temple sacrificial system came to a close, as Jesus predicted (see Matthew 24; Mark 13; Luke 21).

The apostle Peter sums up our irreligious identity in Christ this way: "You also, like living stones, are being built into a spiritual house to be a holy priesthood, offering spiritual sacrifices acceptable to God through Jesus Christ" (1 Peter 2:5). I love this verse. All of us are like "living stones" that make up the structure of God's new temple, where we act as priests to one another and make spiritual sacrifices in how we serve and love one another.

All of the pillars of ancient religion are now summed up in the relational dynamic of God's people living and loving together. This means that the most sacred geography on the planet is not a holy building or a sacred site of religious pilgrimage.

The most sacred space on the planet is the space between you and me when we love one another as Jesus does.

REPLACING RITUALS

James, the half-brother of Jesus, is the only person in the entire Bible to use the word *religion* in an unqualified positive sense when he writes: "Religion that God our Father accepts as pure and faultless is this: to look after orphans and widows in their distress and to keep oneself from being polluted by the world" (James 1:27).

But do you see what he's done here? James talks about pure religion as a way of life that is rooted in love and willing to be countercultural when necessary. For James (and Jesus), the holy places, people, and procedures that make up a typical world religion are not what's important.

The word for religion that James uses here is *threskeia*, and like our English word *religion*, it can be used positively or negatively. *Threskeia* primarily refers to the external behaviors of a religion, including the ceremonies and rituals.

So James is saying that the religious rituals of Christ-followers are no longer things like memorizing religious liturgies, attending religious services, going on religious pilgrimages, celebrating religious holidays, or saying specific prayers at specific times while facing a specific direction in a specific posture. Rather, our rituals are acts of mercy and kindness and compassion, and courage not to take our cues from the world around us. In other words, *our religion is love*.

Jesus changes our concept of religious ritual. Living a holy life that is wholly love—that is our "ritual."

But what about Christian traditions like baptism and the eucharist (or the Lord's Supper or communion, as different Christians call it)?

The difference is *grace*. Christ-followers don't participate in any activity in order to earn what has already been given to us as a gift. Instead, we use certain traditions to *remind us of what is already ours*. These tangible reminders are not a means to receive grace, but a means of celebrating the grace we have already received. And that difference is crucial.

So baptism doesn't save us or cleanse us or remove any sin in and of itself. But it does remind us that we are already cleansed, forgiven, washed, and reborn into a new life by God's gift of grace. The eucharist doesn't get us any more of God's grace than we already have. But it does remind us of how Jesus has loved us to death and of our privilege to receive Christ's love into our very selves. That's the beauty of the tradition—we are physically enacting a spiritual drama, taking "the body and blood of Christ" into our bodies to remind ourselves that we have already received the life essence of Jesus into our souls. "Do this in remembrance of me," said Jesus (Luke 22:19; 1 Corinthians 11:24-25), and so we do it: not in order to achieve something we don't yet possess, but to remember what we already have.

Rituals don't make things true, but they can be wonderful ways to help what *is* true sink deeper into our souls.

REPLACING RULES

Children need rules and routines. Eventually, the goal is to grow to the point of being internally motivated by love to make the wise choice in every situation. Rules function like moral training wheels to keep us alive long enough for our minds to develop and our hearts to learn.

And so, for a season, while humanity was growing up, God gave us a covenant of rules, regulations, rituals, and routines—a way of life that little children need. The religion of Jesus' day was rule-based. Through Moses, God had provided the law: a moral code rooted in, but not limited to, the Ten Commandments. It was meant to serve God's people for a time, but it was never God's ideal, and it was never intended to show us the fullness of God's heart. For that, we needed Jesus: "For the law was given through Moses; grace and truth came through Jesus Christ" (John 1:17; see also Hebrews 7:18-19; Romans 3:21). The old covenant was outside in, a kind of moral exoskeleton designed to keep us moving in the right direction. It was not bad; it was just never meant to be permanent. This law-based living was always meant to be a kind of holding pattern, a kind of nanny to guide us as little children until we became ready for friendship with God (see Galatians 3:23–4:7).

When the time had fully come, through Jesus, God helped us all grow up. Jesus introduced his followers to a new love ethic that would replace their old law ethic, and the Bible says this was what God was moving humankind toward all along.

But first God had to put to death, so to speak, the old covenant of laws. And that's exactly what we see going on in the crucifixion of Jesus. The apostle Paul writes about the death of Jesus as being the end of law: "He nullified in his flesh the law of commandments in decrees . . . through the cross" (Ephesians 2:15-16 NET; see also Colossians 2:13-14).

Centuries before Jesus was born, God had revealed this part of the plan through ancient prophets like Jeremiah. Here we see the hope of a "new covenant," a new way of relating. Jeremiah wrote, "'The days are coming,' declares the Lord, 'when I will make a new covenant with the people of Israel and with the people of Judah. . . . This is the covenant I will make with the people of Israel after that time. . . . I will put my law in their minds and write it on their hearts. I will be their God, and they will be my people. . . . For I will forgive their wickedness and will remember their sins no more'" (Jeremiah 31:31-34).

A new covenant. A new way of being in relationship together. Knowing and being known. Forgiveness and forgetfulness working together to put our sin behind us and give us all a fresh start. What good news!

GOD'S TOP TEN

"But surely the Ten Commandments still endure," some religious people protest. "They were written in stone by the finger of God! That must mean that we should keep them front and center as our guide for life." That's a common sentiment among many Christians who seem to forget that the Ten Commandments are part of the old covenant.

Religious Christians have long tried to have their covenant cake and eat it too by claiming that the Old Testament law (believed to be a total of 613 laws) is divided into three categories—civil, ceremonial, and moral—and that two of these have ended while one endures. Civil law—the law that governs the nation of Israel—doesn't apply to us today, the reasoning goes, since we live in different countries with different leadership structures (i.e., democracies instead of theocracies). Ceremonial law—the law that governs the religious ceremonies of ancient Judaism—is also done away with, since most of it revolves around a purity code and sacrificial system made redundant by the final sacrifice of Jesus. However, God's moral or ethical law—the law that teaches us how to live righteous lives—still endures, because all people of every place and every race and every time and every space are called to follow God's moral standards. And whaddya know: the Ten Commandments fall into this enduring category.

This schema is very neat and tidy, and it seems like a handy way to answer the question of why Christians like to obey some bits of the Bible and not others. But there is a problem: the Old Testament law does not classify itself so clearly. Through Moses,

God presented the old covenant law to Israel as an all-or-nothing deal. In fact, even those Christians who claim that the moral law, like the Ten Commandments, endures and must be obeyed today tend *not* to obey the fourth commandment to keep holy the Sabbath day, which is Saturday. Most Christians follow the lead of the early church and worship on Sundays. As Laurel said to Hardy, this is a fine mess.

When Jesus inaugurated the new covenant—God's new way of relating directly to us through Jesus and his Holy Spirit—he ushered in a new era of love rather than law as our guiding principle. That's why one of the writers of the New Testament calls the Old Testament, including the Ten Commandments, "the ministry that brought death, which was engraved in letters on stone" (2 Corinthians 3:7). In the same passage, we read that God's will is written "not with ink but with the Spirit of the living God, not on tablets of stone but on tablets of human hearts" (2 Corinthians 3:3). Even the Ten Commandments, the only part of the Old Testament law that was written on stone, can't add a thing to what God has done for us through Jesus.

As you can imagine, this idea of annulment—the undoing of the old—has immense implications for how Christians read the Bible. Even though we learn about Jesus *from the Bible*, the Jesus we learn about *in the Bible* would not advocate *following the Bible*. Rather, we read the Bible to learn about the failure of the old and the beauty of the new, brought about by Jesus, who said "Follow me."

LOVE VS. LAW

One of the earliest Christ-followers, the apostle Paul, knew firsthand what it meant to try to follow the old way of the letter of the law. As a leading religious scholar in his day, Paul had dedicated his life to living according to the law of Moses and helping others do the same. His conclusion? Law-based living has the immediate advantage of clarity, but it fails to develop our hearts in the way of love.

Paul wrote, "For when we were in the realm of the flesh, the sinful passions aroused by the law were at work in us, so that we bore fruit for death. But now, by dying to what once bound us, we have been released from the law so that we serve in the new way of the Spirit, and not in the old way of the written code" (Romans 7:5-6).

Sinful passions aroused by the law? That's what law-based living leads to. In the same passage, Paul talks about how being told not to covet (the final of the Ten Commandments) simply made him want to covet all the more! Here are a few more examples of how law-based living fails to inspire the best in us:

When you are standing in an elevator and you notice a sign on the wall that says "Wet Paint—Do Not Touch," what do you immediately want to do?

When daycare centers began to levy fines on parents for being late to pick up their children, the share of parents who were late *increased*.

When an eighteen-month-old toddler sees an adult drop something, she will move to pick it up and hand it back within five seconds. If you repeat the experiment but reward the baby, her tendency toward spontaneous kindness will *decrease*.

The Boston fire department had a longstanding policy of unlimited sick days, and firefighters took the ones they needed on the honor system. When the department imposed a limit of fifteen sick days per year, after which firefighters were docked pay, guess what happened the following year. You're catching the pattern. The number of firefighters who called in sick for holidays like Christmas *increased*—tenfold![6]

And lastly, when a speed *limit* is clearly posted on the highway, what is your goal? If you're like me, your goal is to figure out how far *above* the limit you can go before you get into trouble.

All of these examples highlight one thing: dos and don'ts, musts and mustn'ts, with accompanying rewards and punishments, don't

6. These last three examples are taken from David Brooks, "The Power of Altruism," *New York Times*, July 8, 2016, http://www.nytimes.com/2016/07/08/opinion/the-power-of-altruism.html?_r=0.

make us *want* to behave better. It seems that the way of law diminishes our moral motivation to a contractual arrangement with systems rather than elevate it to a loving attentiveness to persons.

When our family was vacationing in Germany, I had my first opportunity to drive on the autobahn. Many people know this national highway of Germany for one thing—no speed limit. This was going to be a new experience for me, and I was ready to test the limits. (Which wasn't going to be that wild, since we were driving a rented camper.)

As we pulled onto the autobahn for the first time, Nina leaned over and said, "Just remember you love your family." As we got up to cruising speed, something strange happened. I noticed a new idea taking shape in my mind: I was wondering to myself how fast would be safe. For the first time in my life, my driving mind was focused on how fast I *should* go rather than how fast I *could* go.

Love gets you thinking in ways law never can. The new covenant lifts the law, creating space for love to lead.

We're talking about more than changes in driving patterns. In first-century Israel, lifting the law meant the undoing of religion. And that kind of teaching could get a guy killed.

SPEAKING OF GRACE: PAUL

So far in this chapter we've focused on the aspects of religion that Jesus replaces, changes, or simply brings to an end. Now let's talk about the irreligious implications of it all and zero in on one word that sums it all up so well. We'll look at one passage written by the apostle Paul and then one story told by Jesus.

Remember that religion thrives on the idea of an ongoing problem: the need for us to get absolution for sins, or to work off bad karma, or to dispel negative energy, or to fix whatever the religion identifies as the hurdle to overcome. Religion is a cycle of spiritual codependency between us and our system of choice.

But once God gets rid of our sin and guilt once and for all, religion is out of a job. The Bible reminds Christ-followers that they have no need to return to the old way of religion. They truly are free.

This irreligious idea—that God does for us what religion tries but fails to do—is summed up in one amazing word: *grace*. You'll recall that grace was one of our runners-up in "the gospel in one word" competition, and you'll have noticed we've been using the word throughout the book so far. That's because it is simply impossible to talk about the gospel without referring to this radical and extremely irreligious concept. Grace means gift—God's gifts of life, forgiveness, freedom, intimacy, joy, peace, satisfaction, salvation, and everything else religion promises but fails to deliver.

The apostle Paul wrote to his friend Timothy about the all-encompassing power of grace: "He has saved us and called us to a holy life—not because of anything we have done but because of his own purpose and grace. This grace was given us in Christ Jesus before the beginning of time, but it has now been revealed through the appearing of our Savior, Christ Jesus, who has destroyed death and has brought life and immortality to light through the gospel" (2 Timothy 1:9-10).

Notice four things from this passage:

First, God *has saved us* already. You don't have to work for what you already have.

Second, we are called to live *holy* lives. The word *holy* means to be set apart, to be distinct. Holy means we don't have to try to blend in. And the way of grace is definitely distinctive.

Third, this grace was always part of God's plan, even *before the beginning of time*, but this grace waited until Jesus to be fully realized.

Fourth, *Jesus* is at the center of the whirlwind of grace. As Paul says in another letter, "The grace of God has appeared that offers salvation to all people" (Titus 2:11). Jesus is God's grace appearing, becoming visible, tangible, and relatable to all.

Paul was a grace guru. He loved the gospel of grace and took every opportunity to champion the radical, irreligious idea that God gives us directly what religion tries but fails to achieve.

In one famous passage, Paul says, "For the wages of sin is death, but the gift of God is eternal life in Christ Jesus our Lord"

(Romans 6:23). What a statement of contrasts! Life is contrasted with death, which makes sense. But in a stunning irreligious twist, wages are contrasted with a free gift. In essence, Paul is saying, "If sin was a job that you worked hard at every day, then the wages that you earned—your pay on payday—would be death." But notice that God doesn't invite you to switch jobs in order to work for him so you can *earn* life instead of death. Paul didn't say, "For the wages of sin is death, but the wages of working for God is eternal life." No! That would be the way of religion. Rather, through Jesus, God *gives* you life as a gift of grace.

If grace is true, then there is nothing left to be done in order to get on God's good side. We can rest in the knowledge that God is for us, not against us. He proves this through Jesus, who loves humanity to death, and rises again to forgive us—even for killing him.

Religion thrives by keeping us on our toes regarding what will happen to us when we die. Will God judge us harshly? Will we have amassed enough good deeds to break free of our karmic cycle? Or will we have to return to suffer more? Will we be sent to hell? Will we be assessed in detail, with all our sins dredged up for discussion?

Grace says that we don't need to wait until judgment day to find out how it will go for us. Because God gives us eternal life as a gift, here and now, we can move confidently into our future as people who *are already* saved, *already* justified, *already* made right with God.

SPEAKING OF GRACE: JESUS

Jesus is described as "full of grace" (John 1:14) and called "the appearing of God's grace" (see Titus 2:11), but nowhere is it recorded that Jesus ever used the word *grace*. Because of that, sometimes people think that grace is a concept invented by the apostle Paul and other early church leaders rather than Jesus. That kind of thinking misses something crucial: in his stories and his relationships, Jesus taught and modeled grace over and over. He didn't have to use the word because he lived it out every day.

One of my favorite parables of Jesus is all about grace:

For the kingdom of heaven is like a landowner who went out early in the morning to hire workers for his vineyard. He agreed to pay them a denarius for the day and sent them into his vineyard.

About nine in the morning he went out and saw others standing in the marketplace doing nothing. He told them, "You also go and work in my vineyard, and I will pay you whatever is right." So they went.

He went out again about noon and about three in the afternoon and did the same thing. About five in the afternoon he went out and found still others standing around. He asked them, "Why have you been standing here all day long doing nothing?"

"Because no one has hired us," they answered.

He said to them, "You also go and work in my vineyard."

When evening came, the owner of the vineyard said to his foreman, "Call the workers and pay them their wages, beginning with the last ones hired and going on to the first."

The workers who were hired about five in the afternoon came and each received a denarius. So when those came who were hired first, they expected to receive more. But each one of them also received a denarius. When they received it, they began to grumble against the landowner. "These who were hired last worked only one hour," they said, "and you have made them equal to us who have borne the burden of the work and the heat of the day."

But he answered one of them, "I am not being unfair to you, friend. Didn't you agree to work for a denarius? Take your pay and go. I want to give the one who was hired last the same as I gave you. Don't I have the right to do what I want with my own money? Or are you envious because I am generous?"

So the last will be first, and the first will be last. (Matthew 20:1-16)

Four things in this parable stand out. First, notice that Jesus said this is a story about the "kingdom of heaven," or what he often called the "kingdom of God." God's kingdom is a kingdom of grace.

Second, the landowner, representing God in this story, partners with common people to get his work done. Paul called us "God's co-workers" (2 Corinthians 6:1). God wants you to join his cause, to make a difference. He doesn't just want spectators, worshipers, cheerleaders, or people who will praise him while he does it all. He wants partners, coworkers, and world changers who will work with him.

Third, the landowner chooses his workers on the basis of grace, not qualification. The only qualification, if we can even call it that, is that you show up: that you say yes. The landowner doesn't just select the biggest and the best, the youngest and strongest. He chooses whoever is in need of work and willing to work. God hates to see people wasting their lives away when they could be accomplishing great things.

Fourth, the landowner is amazingly gracious in his pay. He goes beyond what is fair to what is exceedingly, excessively, preposterously kind. He is so gracious that he busts any normal business boundaries. It's as if he's gone a tad crazy, like the transformed Ebenezer Scrooge on Christmas morning. In fact, he is so kind that some people get upset.

But notice why people are thrown off. It's not because God is a miser or a tyrant, and not because he is too demanding or judgmental. People get upset because he is too kind! Jesus seems to be saying that God is so loving, so gracious, so generous that if you put him into a human context, he would appear crazy with kindness.

If you are a very religious person who has worked long and hard to achieve some sort of spiritual reward, you could be scandalized by this irrational grace. If you are a religious leader stewarding a system that teaches people to work for their heavenly reward, this teaching might seem threatening, because it undermines your current system of salvation. This is exactly what happened with Jesus: the religious leaders of his day became so threatened by his message of grace that they eventually plotted to have him executed.

So when we define the gospel in ways that make God appear crazy with kindness and radically inclusive—even to the point of scandalizing religious conservatives—we are on the right track.

BECOMING WHO YOU REALLY ARE

Wouldn't you love the chance to start life over again? To have the innocence of youth without losing the wisdom of age? At the risk of sounding like a skin cream commercial—now you can!

Jesus talked about life with him being a complete restart, like being born into a whole new life, complete with an entirely new identity (see John 3:1-17). One benefit of this idea is that you can learn how to *live* like a new person and *love* like a new person when you realize that you actually *are* a new person. And the early church took him at his word.

To a group of Christians who were losing sight of their new God-given identity and were returning to their old lives of sin and selfishness, the apostle Paul wrote out a long list of the kinds of sins they were dealing with, and then he added, "And that is what some of you *were*. But you *were* washed, you *were* sanctified, you *were* justified in the name of the Lord Jesus Christ and by the Spirit of our God" (1 Corinthians 6:11). Were. Were. Were. Were. All past tense.

When we say yes to Jesus, we are no longer defined by the failures of our past. Neither are we defined by the failures of our present. When we mess up again, the solution isn't to judge and condemn each other, but to remind each other of who we were—and even better, who we truly *are*. Our past may continue to lie to us and tell us that we are no better than the sum total of our mistakes. But through a regular renewing of our minds with the gospel, through the memory of our baptism, and through the ongoing celebration of the Lord's Supper, we can remind ourselves of who we really are.

THE CHRISTIAN RELIGION

But what about our original question? If Jesus came to shut down religion, why did he end up starting one of the world's biggest religions instead? The quick answer is that he didn't. We did.

It is our ongoing human impulse to systematize faith and then worship the system. Our weak hearts bend toward idolatry because it is more concrete, predictable, and immediate. After seeing God's miracles and hearing God's voice, Israel still built the golden calf the first chance they got. After seeing God heal people through the bronze serpent, Israel started worshiping *it* instead of God. And after Jesus provided the last sacrifice and proclaimed the end of religion, it didn't take long for people to say, "What a terrific message—let's build a religion out of that!" And so it goes.

Each new generation will be tempted to settle for something less than the glorious gospel of union with the Almighty, and instead build a religion out of a lesser, truncated message. The possibility of diversion will always be present because our relationship with God, like all relationships, will benefit from the help of traditions, routines, special places, boundaries, and guidelines. And because these kinds of things can and do serve a good relationship, sometimes we will become lazy and turn to the things themselves to sustain us. Sometimes we will go through the motions but miss the heartbeat of friendship with God, "having a form of godliness but denying its power" (2 Timothy 3:5).[7]

This is why the gospel is more than a message we are saved by and then can move on from. The gospel is a message all people need, including those of us who have been enjoying life with God for many years.[8]

---

7. For a more expansive discussion of the positive and negative contributions of tradition and ritual, see chapters 3 and 8 in my book *The End of Religion.*
8. Again, let me stress that some people will talk about their vivid, joyful, and faith-filled relationship with God as them being very "religious," and here we simply acknowledge that we are using our words differently. Happens all the time. The important thing is that, whatever words we use, we learn and live the gospel of salvation by grace through faith.

BEGINNING, MIDDLE, END

When we read the opening chapters of the Bible and see the world
God created before we humans had a chance to mess it up, we
notice something significant: there is no "religion." There are no
special places where Adam and Eve need to go to meet with God,
no special rituals they need to participate in to make God appear
or to receive his favor, and no special leaders needed to mediate
between them and God. There is just God and humanity living
together in naked intimacy.

The same holds true for the closing chapters of the Bible. At
the end of the book of Revelation, we find that God is bringing
us back to the same kind of living. A reunion, in which we know
God with no religion.

Sandwiched in between, in the middle of it all, there is Jesus,
helping humanity to spiritually course correct by reconnecting us
to our Source and our Goal. If we are willing to trust Jesus, he will
lead us directly into the center of God's love life.

11
GOD'S LOVE LIFE

*God became what we are, that He
might bring us to be what He is.*
—IRENAEUS (EARLY SECOND CENTURY CE)

JESUS IS GOD WITH US, COME TO

SHOW US GOD'S LOVE,	SAVE US FROM SIN,	SET UP GOD'S KINGDOM, AND	SHUT DOWN RELIGION,

SO WE CAN **SHARE IN GOD'S LIFE.**

Speaking of God, the ancient philosopher Epimenides said: "In him we live and move and have our being."[1] God is the spiritual oxygen that keeps us alive every day. But too often we hold our breath.

Jesus said that he came to give us life, eternal and abundant (John 10:10). God wants to share his life with us, and that life

---

1. Epimenides was a sixth-century BCE Greek poet-philosopher; he is speaking here specifically about Zeus. The apostle Paul said Epimenides was right about Ultimate Reality, even if he was wrong about the name (see Acts 17:28). This reminds us that we can find partial truth about God everywhere, in every religion and every philosophy, and should eagerly keep our eyes open for it, while simultaneously filtering what we learn through the pure, undiluted truth of Jesus.

is pure love. We were made *by* love, made *to* love, and made *for* love—a life of love with God and one another. This is *the goal of the gospel*. Theologians use the word *theosis* to refer to the goal of the gospel: becoming (re)united with God. Theosis is a *re*union because we have wandered away from and want to return to the intimacy we once had in the garden of Eden. But it is also a *new* union in its own right, because through the incarnation, God has bonded with humanity so that we can bond with him to form an intimate union that surpasses the intimacy we experienced in the garden of Eden.

Before Nina and I were married, we lived apart for a year. Nina was living in Zambia, assessing whether to make a career overseas as a primary healthcare nurse. I stayed in Canada, committed to my pastoral role at The Meeting House. It was a painful, though productive, year. And when she returned, it was a beautiful reunion for the two of us.

But this reunion wasn't the end of our story—it was just the beginning. When we were married, it was more than a *re*union, but a new, deeper, richer *union*. We were back together, but we weren't going back; we were moving forward into something even better. As the preacher said at our wedding, "And the two shall become one flesh."

This is the story arc of humankind's relationship with God. We were together. We went away (and not for a good reason). And now, upon our return, things will be even better; they will be closer and more intimate than they were at the beginning. The intimacy of marriage, including the joy of sexual union, is a living picture of God's desire to bring us into complete union with himself.

WHERE THE STREETS HAVE NO NAME

If I were to ask a group of church folk what the goal of the gospel is, many of them might say something like, "To get us into heaven when we die." And that wouldn't be entirely wrong. Certainly the biblical writers use the term *heaven* to speak of the destiny of those who are "in Christ."

But the Bible also gives us clues that what we call heaven is less of a *place* and more of a *Person*. That is, *heaven* is shorthand for our eternal life lived within God's own love life.

When God gave the apostle John a vision of heaven in the book of Revelation, John described what he saw in vivid and symbolic detail. A celestial city? Check. Streets of gold? Check. Pearly gates? Check.

But in the middle of describing heaven as a city, John says something very revealing: "I did not see a temple in the city, because the Lord God Almighty and the Lamb are its temple" (Revelation 21:22). The absence of a temple in heaven has irreligious implications. No temple means no sacrifice and no religious system. Just pure, undiluted intimacy with the Almighty.

A temple is a place where a deity's presence is thought to dwell in some special way. Ancient people would enter temples to meet with the divine. Now notice that John doesn't say that heaven is the temple where we will meet God. Instead, John says that *God himself is the temple*. What we call "heaven" is scriptural short form for our eternal life *in God*.

The good news of the gospel just keeps getting better and better.

THE STORY OF GLORY

Through the gospel, God wants to bring us into a new way of being human—a new way of living now and forever that is permeated by and participating in the glorious love life of God.

One of the attributes that sets God above and beyond all other persons, things, or concepts is his absolute glory. The Greek word for glory (*doxa*) means both heaviness and radiance. God is "heavy," not in physical weight, but heavy in meaning and significance—as in "Whoa . . . that's heavy, man." We could say that to speak of God's "glory" is to speak of his awesomeness, his absolute transcendence.

This glory of God is the totality of what sets him apart, the purity and power of his undiluted, creative love shining to and through all creation (Isaiah 6:3). God created us *for his own* glory

(Isaiah 43:7), and yet, what is most surprising, the Bible says that God also wants to share his glory with us.

We were made to share in and radiate the glory of God, but we walked away from our calling early on in our existence, and now we all fall short of the glory of God (Romans 3:23). But God hasn't given up on sharing the treasure of his full glory with us (John 17:22; 2 Corinthians 3:18; 4:6-7; Romans 8:17-21). God doesn't want spectators, he wants participants. He wants partners. This vision of sharing his glory with his image-bearers is what gives God hope, what makes God happy, and what motivated Jesus to endure the cross to make a way for our reunion with God.

An ancient Christian author wrote this about Jesus: "For the joy set before him he endured the cross, scorning its shame, and sat down at the right hand of the throne of God" (Hebrews 12:2). I used to think that the "joy set before him" probably meant his resurrection. I thought that Jesus found the strength to endure the suffering of crucifixion because he knew that in a couple of days he would be back again to rub it in their faces and say one big, fat "I'm back, suckers!" But my friend Josh helped me think this through in line with the relational emphasis of Jesus. The "joy set before him" that helped Jesus endure the cross was you. And me. The joy of Jesus, even in the midst of his most excruciating pain, has always been the (re)union he would one day have with us.

God is committed to a joyful union with us that includes sharing his own glory. We are already experiencing a measure of this *glorification* here and now as God's heirs and co-heirs with Christ (Romans 8:17-21), and one day we will experience this joyful intimacy without hindrance or distraction. For those who give their life over to Jesus, the best is always yet to come.

WHERE DO "I" GO?

So does this vision of glorious divine-human intimacy mean we will be absorbed into God and lose our individual identities after we die? Will we be like drops of water falling into the ocean of deity, or like broken eggs mixed into some sort of cosmic ontological omelet?

No. Our life "in God" is a life of love, and love exists within the reality of individuated *persons in relationship*.

Think of the incarnation of Christ. When Jesus became human, he did not cease to be divine. Nor did he cease to be the person he always was. He was not absorbed into some concept of cosmic humanity like a drop of deity falling into the ocean of humankind. Jesus retained his own personhood while simultaneously merging that divine personhood with our humanity. This is a paradigm for our journey into God's love life. We will not be absorbed into God in a way that cancels out our humanity or our identity. Rather, we will be ourselves, but ourselves caught up in the love life of God: made complete, existing the way we were always meant to be.

That love life with God can begin in this life. The apostle Paul wrote, "I have been crucified with Christ and I no longer live, but Christ lives in me. The life I now live in the body, I live by faith in the Son of God, who loved me and gave himself for me" (Galatians 2:20). The Greek word for "I" is *ego*, and here we see both the loss of ego in one sense—"I have been crucified" and "I no longer live"—and the continuation of the ego in another, purified sense—"the life I now live" and "I live by faith."

Paul's appreciation of God's love was profoundly personal and intensely individual—"who loved *me* and gave himself for *me*." He knew that Jesus doesn't dissolve our true selves or assimilate us into God like some divine version of the Borg. The life of Christ in Paul, energizing his daily living—"Christ lives in me"—meant that he was becoming his true self in union with God.

And what begins in this life will consummate in the next life, when we experience what the Bible calls "the resurrection." The resurrection is not just our way of talking about what happened to Jesus after he died, but what will one day happen to us too. Our eventual resurrection will be patterned on the resurrection of Jesus. While the *death* of Jesus inaugurated the new covenant, it is the ongoing *life* of Jesus that infuses us with life now, and forever.

Let's sift through the dimensions of the new life that Jesus brings: from resurrection and new birth (with baptism as their symbol) to sharing in God's familial life, eternal life, abundant life, and love life. This vision offers us hope for the future, and it also has implications for how we live in the present.

RESURRECTION:
GOD'S GREAT EXCLAMATION POINT

Once a year, Christians all around the globe gather on Easter Sunday to celebrate the resurrection of Jesus. In many churches, people take a moment for a responsive declaration. The pastor proclaims, "He is risen!" And the people respond, "He is risen indeed!" In some churches, this back-and-forth interaction becomes the standard greeting for the day. Instead of "Hello" and "How are you today?" parishioners greet each other with "He is risen!" and respond with "He is risen indeed!"

Indeed! The resurrection of Jesus is God's great exclamation point at the end of Easter weekend; God's way of validating the message, mission, and meaning of Jesus' life and death. Because of the resurrection, Jesus' message of love would now stand as forever authorized, authenticated, and endorsed by God himself. It's like the voice at the end of one of those political ads: "I am Yahweh, and I approve this message."

But Christ's resurrection showed the world more than God's endorsement of Jesus' mission and message. It also shows us a glimpse of God's goal for our future. Jesus said, "Because I live, you also will live" (John 14:19). The apostle Paul taught that Christ's resurrection provided a prototype for what all his followers would one day experience, what he called the "firstfruits" of what we along with all creation can look forward to (e.g., 1 Corinthians 15:20, 23; Romans 8:17-21). So we can look at the resurrection of Jesus to see something of our own destiny. And what do we see?

The resurrection of Jesus, and eventually of us, is not merely a resuscitation: a body coming back to life for a duration of time until finally dying again. Neither is it a transmutation or transmigration: a soul leaving the body behind in order to enter a new plane of existence. Remember, on Easter morning the tomb was empty; Christ's body was gone; it had been changed, not abandoned. The resurrection, then, is a bold statement that body and soul belong together, even if both need to go through a purifying transformation. This is why, at the end of his earthly story, Jesus didn't just disappear, fade away, or become an invisible spirit. Instead, Jesus remained embodied as he returned to the Father (Luke 24:50-52; Acts 1:9-11).

The resurrection and ascension of Jesus demonstrated that God's goal for us isn't eternal life in an ethereal heaven as disembodied spirit beings. No, when God made humans, he made us as spiritual-physical unions, and the biblical promise of resurrection affirms that a continued embodied existence is our eternal destiny (see, e.g., John 5:28-29).

Resurrection affirms that God values the physical. The faith of Jesus is not a gnostic escapism that holds out the hope of one day shuffling off this mortal coil so we can finally be rid of our earthly existence. When God originally created us, including our bodies, he said it was "very good" (Genesis 1:31). God's goal for us is not the rejection of our bodies but "the redemption of our bodies" (Romans 8:23). God loves the world, and he loves us as embodied beings living in this world, and his goal is to renew all things, in heaven and on earth.

Your body is good. Maybe not perfect. Maybe far from totally healthy. But good. Not shameful, not evil, and certainly not disposable.

And what's more, just as Jesus' resurrection is a prototype for what we all can look forward to, our bodily resurrection will be a kind of firstfruits of what all creation will one day experience. The world will not be discarded but renewed. That's why when we read of the culmination of all history, we read that the "New Jerusalem" (that's heaven) comes down to earth, and not the other way around.

See how the apostle John describes his vision of the climax of history in the book of Revelation:

Then I saw "a new heaven and a new earth," for the first heaven and the first earth had passed away, and there was no longer any sea.[2] I saw the Holy City, the new Jerusalem, coming down out of heaven from God, prepared as a bride beautifully dressed for her husband. And I heard a loud voice from the throne saying, "Look! God's dwelling place is now among the people, and he will dwell with them. They will be his people, and God himself will be with them and be their God. 'He will wipe every tear from their eyes. There will be no more death' or mourning or crying or pain, for the old order of things has passed away."

He who was seated on the throne said, "I am making everything new!" Then he said, "Write this down, for these words are trustworthy and true."

He said to me: "It is done. I am the Alpha and the Omega, the Beginning and the End. To the thirsty I will give water without cost from the spring of the water of life. (Revelation 21:1-6)

God will remake and renew all things. Life with God, in God. What a beautiful picture of the goal of the gospel!

REBIRTH: WHEN JESUS CHANGES TIME ZONES

Once, when talking about the resurrection of all people, Jesus changed time zones.

It happened for him mid-thought. "Very truly I tell you, a time is coming *and has now come* when the dead will hear the voice of the Son of God and those who hear will live" (John 5:25). Notice the time change.

Jesus went through a time warp once before when he was talking with a Samaritan woman. This was a triple scandal: he was talking with a Samaritan, he was talking with a woman, and he was unchaperoned. Jesus was telling her about the irreligious nature of the new age of the Spirit. In that conversation he said, "A time is coming *and has now come* when the true worshipers

---

2. In ancient times, the sea was a symbol of mystery, turmoil, separation, and loss. Many ships went to sea and never returned.

will worship the Father in the Spirit and in truth" (John 4:23). Again, notice the time shift. It's as though Jesus could see her faith forming mid-sentence. "The time is coming"—he looked at her face and saw her light up with the awareness of God's intimacy—"and has now come!"

I wonder if that moment might be happening to you as you read this book. A time is coming—and has now come!—when you will fall in love with Jesus. Every new life has a beginning, and Jesus called the start of our forever life with God being "born again" (or "born from above"; see John 3:1-17). What an amazing image this is—the chance to have a fresh start as a newly made person!

Evangelical Christians have often called themselves "born again" Christians, and sometimes our experience with "born againers" has not been positive. (Maybe they need to be born again *again?*) But don't let this powerful spiritual analogy be ruined for you by misaligned religious zealotry or hypocrisy. There is something wonderful for us to see here, and it would be a shame to miss it.

The gospel has the power to completely remake people and give them a fresh start in life, now. Through Christ, everyone can be forgiven, have their slate wiped clean, and be empowered to live loving lives.

The analogy of rebirth was not original to Jesus, but the way he used it was stunning. World religions had long used the symbol of rebirth to speak of our transition from this life to the next— whether that next life meant heaven, nirvana, or reincarnation. The idea of rebirth in religion is usually reserved for something that happens after we die—we are reborn into the afterlife, or reborn into a new earthly life.

But Jesus used the idea of rebirth in a thoroughly Jewish way to refer to an experience of new life right here and now.

This doesn't mean that we start to live perfect, spiritually mature lives free from all failure. But it does mean that our spirit, our center, is remade, cleansed, and empowered here and now.

The first generation of Christ-followers believed they had *already* entered into eternal life. They had *already* died to their old lives and been reborn into better ones. The apostle Peter wrote, "Praise be to the God and Father of our Lord Jesus Christ! In his great mercy he *has given* us new birth into a living hope through the resurrection of Jesus Christ from the dead, and into an inheritance that can never perish, spoil or fade" (1 Peter 1:3-4; see also 1 Peter 1:23).

Since the first generation of Christ-followers, this beautiful truth has been symbolized through baptism—being plunged into water. Going down into the waters of baptism and rising again captured the essence of spiritual rebirth beautifully—being buried, cleansed, and rising to a new life, all happening now.

Water baptism wasn't considered a magical ceremony but a symbol of a deeper reality: *Spirit* baptism (Matthew 3:11; 1 Corinthians 12:13). Like the wedding ring, which doesn't make you married but does symbolize your committed love, water baptism is a symbol of being plunged into God. Baptism says "I'm burying my old life with all its failure and pain, I'm accepting God's cleansing and newness, and I'm coming up out of these waters as a new person, reborn into a better version of myself."

Baptism became a point of reference for Christ-followers, pointing them toward and reminding them of their new identity, new intimacy, and new inclusion.

ADOPTION: LIFE AS FAMILY

Calling God our Father as Jesus taught us isn't just some Middle Eastern sign of respect. In fact, this was not common within the Jewish religion but something Jesus introduced and emphasized. Using the term *Father* for God was considered disrespectful because it made God sound too familiar, too intimate. Religion does tend to emphasize God's transcendence, God being "out there." But Jesus also emphasized God's immanence—God being "right here" as our loving Father. Jesus didn't borrow the analogy of fatherhood from our human families. Rather, calling God our

Father was a way of saying that the whole idea of family comes from God in the first place.

The apostle Paul once referred to God as "the Father, from whom every family in heaven and on earth derives its name" (Ephesians 3:14-15). Do you see? God didn't borrow the idea *from* us; he has loaned his idea *to* us! Life with God is family life.

As we've already covered, we become new members of God's family when we are *born* into our new life in Christ (John 3:1-17; 1 Peter 1:22-23). But the early Christian community also used another metaphor to expand our understanding of our new family life with God. They used the idea of *adoption* to help communicate how we move from individual life into family-styled spiritual life through Christ.

> For those who are led by the Spirit of God are the children of God. The Spirit you received does not make you slaves, so that you live in fear again; rather, the Spirit you received brought about your adoption to sonship.[3] And by him we cry, "*Abba* [italics in original], Father." The Spirit himself testifies with our spirit that we are God's children. Now if we are children, then we are heirs—heirs of God and co-heirs with Christ, if indeed we share in his sufferings in order that we may also share in his glory. (Romans 8:14-17; see also Galatians 4:1-7)

When we trust in Jesus, he gives us his Spirit. And the Holy Spirit pulls us into the family life of God as God's children. Inside us, God's Spirit moves us to relate to God as our Abba, which is more than the name of a cheesy Swedish disco group. *Abba* is the Aramaic word for "Dad" or "Daddy"—a term of intimacy and trust used by little children toward their father.

And we become co-heirs with Christ! That sounds amazing, but what does it mean? What inheritance does Jesus receive from

---

3. The image of sonship in this Romans passage might sound exclusionary toward women, but the opposite is true here. Back in biblical times, only sons could receive an inheritance. Daughters got nothing. To say that men and women could be adopted into "sonship" with God was a way of championing equality. That is, both women and men could equally look forward to the full blessings of inheritance from God.

God? The only thing that the Bible describes passing down from the Father to the Son is the glory of the Father's affirmation, intimacy, pleasure, and love (Luke 3:22; John 17:26). *This* is the inheritance of Christ. And this is now *our* inheritance as well. We are placed on par with Jesus as his brothers and sisters (Romans 8:29), ready to receive the same measure of our Father's love.

Having God as our Father means that we can relate to each other as sisters and brothers beyond the poetry of the imagery (1 Timothy 5:1-2). Members of the early church related to each other as brother and sister not because it was *symbolically* true, but because it was *actually* true, as brought about by God's Spirit.

If blood is thicker than water, then spirit is thicker than blood.

ETERNAL LIFE:
STARTING FOREVER HERE AND NOW

Jesus said, "Very truly I tell you, whoever hears my word and believes him who sent me *has* eternal life and will not be judged but *has crossed over* from death to life" (John 5:24). And again, "Very truly I tell you, the one who believes *has* eternal life" (John 6:47).

See that? Jesus didn't promise that one day we will have eternal life; he said when we trust him (that means to simply receive by faith the gift of salvation by grace), we have eternal life. We *have already crossed over* into the life that lasts forever. Our judgment day is already past and we have been justified, and so we have already begun the business of living forever. This is cause for celebration!

In fact, spiritually speaking, God already sees us as living now with Jesus in heaven. We're as good as there! The apostle Paul makes this clear: "Like the rest, we were by nature deserving of wrath. But because of his great love for us, God, who is rich in mercy, *made us alive with Christ* even when we were dead in transgressions—it is by grace you *have been* saved. And *God raised us up with Christ and seated us with him in the heavenly realms in Christ Jesus*, in order that in the coming ages he might show the incomparable riches of his grace, expressed in his kindness to us in Christ Jesus" (Ephesians 2:3-7).

And in another passage: "Since, then, *you have been raised* with Christ, set your hearts on things above, where Christ is, seated at the right hand of God. Set your minds on things above, not on earthly things. For *you died and your life is now hidden with Christ in God*. When *Christ, who is your life*, appears, then you also will appear with him in glory" (Colossians 3:1-4).

Your life is now hidden with Christ in God. I have a strange mental image when I read this phrase. I picture our Saint Bernard, George, digging in the dirt for his bone. When George knows the taste he wants is in that bone, and that the bone he wants is buried in the ground, he digs with all his puppy power and doggy determination. This is how I want to be with God. My life, the life I want, the life I desire to live here and now—this life is to be found in Christ, who is in God. And I'm going to direct all my energy in that direction.

Because of this, I want to live each day with my mind *set on things above*. That doesn't mean we ignore what is going on in the world around us. Quite the contrary. To set our minds on things above means that we put Jesus first, his mind first, his perspective first—and Jesus teaches us how to look at the world around us with a fresh sense of compassion, empathy, and involvement.

This also means that we can begin now to live the life that lasts forever—our eternal life now. What kind of life do you want to live into eternity?

A life of love? Start living a loving life now.

A life of peace? Start living a life of peace now.

A life of intimacy? Start drawing closer to God and others, reconciling broken relationships now.

A life of celebration? Let's get this party started!

DIVINE LIFE: ENTERING THE HEART OF GOD

Let me quote that wise sage and spiritual guru, Yoda, as he speaks to Luke Skywalker about the Force in *The Empire Strikes Back*: "My ally is the Force. And a powerful ally it is. . . . Its energy surrounds us, and binds us. . . . You must feel the Force around you—here, between you, me, the tree, the rock, everywhere."

Yoda is pointing us in the right direction, but the full truth is even better. This "Force" that permeates everything is *personal*. And more than personal, this Force is *relational*. And Jesus came to, among other things, guide us into a conscious and fully engaged relationship with this Force of Love.

The apostle Peter wrote: "His divine power has given us everything we need for a godly life through our knowledge of him who called us by his own glory and goodness. Through these he has given us his very great and precious promises, so that through them *you may participate in the divine nature*, having escaped the corruption in the world caused by evil desires" (2 Peter 1:3-4).

To participate in the divine nature: this is the goal of the gospel. Literally, to have ongoing fellowship, intimate interaction, with God's own inherent disposition, his divine essence, which we know is love—the actual relational *love life* of the Holy Trinity.

And notice the last phrase of those verses: *having escaped the corruption in the world caused by evil desires*. The word *evil* is not in the original Greek text, but has been added by the translators for clarity. Peter's point here is that one day all our desires, which are often evil because they grow out of hearts that are unsatisfied and ungrateful, will be satisfied. We will no longer be distracted by the decay of the world, the destruction of nature, and the dismantling of relationships, which are all caused by our ungrateful lust for more. We will have more. We will be more. We will love more.

LOVE LIFE: INFINITE INTIMACY

When Jesus taught about this eternal, abundant, divine life at the Last Supper, he first washed his disciples' feet, showing them the way of other-centered love. Then he began to teach them about the goal of the gospel: our inclusion in the love life of God. Jesus said:

> If you love me, keep my commands. And I will ask the Father, and he will give you another advocate to help you and be with you forever—the Spirit of truth. The world cannot accept him,

because it neither sees him nor knows him. But you know him, for he lives with you and will be in you. I will not leave you as orphans; I will come to you. Before long, the world will not see me anymore, but you will see me. Because I live, you also will live. On that day you will realize that I am in my Father, and you are in me, and I am in you. (John 14:15-20)

What intimacy! Jesus will ask the Father, and the Father will send the Spirit, and the Spirit will so represent the mind of Christ that Jesus can say "*I* will be *with* you, and will be *in* you."[4]

And what's more, while we have Jesus in us, Jesus says we are also invited into Jesus. The early Christians often referred to themselves as being "in Christ" (e.g., Romans 8:1; 1 Corinthians 1:30; 2 Corinthians 5:17; Galatians 3:28; Ephesians 2:13; 1 Peter 5:14). It was their way of relationally locating themselves in their new identity. This identity was as real to them as me saying that I am "in Canada," which I am as I write this. But being "in Christ" says more about me than my nationality, my ethnicity, my gender, or my status. It is an identity of complete intimacy.

Through Jesus' physical life on earth he was "Immanuel," God with us. But through the Holy Spirit, he is God with us *and within* us. And us within him.

It gets better. If we are in Jesus, then—and this blows my mind—when Jesus returns to the Father to experience reunion with God, he takes us all with him, into him. Our eternal destiny is to live within Christ in God.

But we don't have to wait for this astounding intimacy with the Almighty. Jesus goes on to specify that *the Father* himself will come and dwell within his followers (John 14:23). This is the full life of the Trinity, living relationally within us now.

Then, when Jesus is talking with the Father, we get to hear him say, "I have made you known to them, and will continue to make you known in order that the love you have for me may be in them

---

4. See also John 14:26; 15:26; 16:12-15; 1 Corinthians 2:16; Galatians 4:19; Colossians 1:27. This idea that the members of the Trinity interpenetrate one another so that to know one is to know all is called the doctrine of *perichoresis*.

and that I myself may be in them" (John 17:26). Understanding this one verse of Scripture can change our internal experience forever. Jesus not only restates that *he* will be in us (along with the Father and the Spirit), but here also specifies that *the love the Father has for Jesus* will also be within us.

Jesus says that the very dynamic of the love relationship he has with the Father—that is, the very energy of love that passes between them—will dwell within us. Jesus wants us to be filled with not only the presence of God, but also an ongoing experience of the love that flows between the persons of the Trinity. It isn't just the *person* of God who comes to dwell within us. It is the *relationship* of God that comes to dwell within us.

Remember the most basic reality of all—"God is love" (1 John 4:8, 16). And love is not merely a philosophical concept or a static energy that hovers "out there" in an idea cloud. Love is a dynamic experience between persons, a form of relating that is self-giving, always exalting in the honor of another. Love may begin as an intention *within* a person, but if it only remains an intention, then it stagnates as mere sentiment. For love to actually be love, it must become expressed *between* persons. For God to be love, God's basic essence must be made up of persons relating.

So Jesus is the one who opens the door for us to experience not only God's love *for us*, but also the love of God within God that the members of the Trinity have *for each other*. Now we can live every moment of every day surrounded by, infused with, and engaged with the actual love relationship that we call "God."

AN INCUBATOR OF AGAPE

Years ago I went through a season of significant loss. Many areas of my world came crashing down all at once—family life, work life, emotional life. For many months I needed friendship, but I didn't have the capacity to *be* a friend. Sometimes I cried all day. Other days my grief overwhelmed me to the point that I'd become emotionally numb and unable to do anything but sit and stare.

My emotional world needed to be rebuilt, reassembled, and reenergized, but many days I didn't have the capacity to engage with the very people who might help me in that process.

That's when I met Greg. Greg would eventually become my best friend (which is doubly true, since his last name is Best). Greg offered me patient and kind friendship, but he also offered something more. Greg welcomed me into the life of his family. The Best family made space for me—sometimes to fully participate as an adopted family member, playing games and enjoying conversation, and other times to just sit and let their family life happen around me. There were days when all I could do was sit on the couch and stare at the floor while the kids played and Greg and Chris, his wife, chatted with each other. In that environment, where love flowed back and forth between Greg, Chris, Daniel, and Michelle, I began to heal.

When I was unable to fully give or receive love in any significant fashion, I was still being nourished by love. In the Best home, I was surrounded by family life and family love flowing between them and including me to the extent I was ready for, day by day, moment by moment.

In that incubator of agape love, my soul and my psyche grew in health and hope. And for me, this will always be a picture of the goal of the gospel.

The good news is that all of us are invited into God's own agape circle, called the Trinity. This is our destiny by design. And because our eternal life starts now, we can begin to cultivate this relational intimacy on this side of heaven. It all starts with the simple awareness the gospel brings: God is with you right now, wanting you to know just how much you are loved.

God has made room in his heart for us because he has made us valuable to himself. In Luke 15, Jesus tells three stories of three lost things—the lost coin, the lost sheep, and the lost son. Each of the lost things have this in common: they were valuable to the one who had lost them.

You are valuable to God—so valuable, in fact, that God has gone to extreme lengths to bring you into his love life. Through Jesus, God made room for humankind to be a part of his own intimate fellowship. When Jesus came to earth, "the Word *became* flesh" (John 1:14). God *became*. Think about that. God was willing to alter his own qualities to become something he had never been. In Christ, God proved that humanity and deity are compatible. In Christ, God and humankind are *united*. And in Christ, God has now taken that humanity up into his own self.

Jesus did not shed his humanity when he ascended to heaven (1 Timothy 2:5). He did not reject but redeemed his humanity—and ours. Yes, Jesus is God. And now, Jesus is eternally human too. Through Christ, humanity is now and forever will be an aspect, an element, a quality of who God is.

So there is room in God for humankind. Jesus has led the way.

12

THE F-WORD

Never be afraid to trust an unknown future to a known God.
—CORRIE TEN BOOM

It's busy in my brain. Ever since I was a child I've lived a lot of life in my head: always questioning, always puzzling, always wondering. Some philosophers call this a "reflective mind": a mind that habitually turns over the mental stones of every conceptual landscape to find the creepy crawlies underneath.

Whenever I make a choice, the first thing I do is question that choice. I doubt every decision. When I decide what line to stand in at the grocery store checkout, I immediately create a series of virtual Bruxys to stand in every other line. Then I keep track of which Bruxy made the best line choice for the quickest exit from the store. I've always done this, whether choosing what degree to get, what career to pursue, or what lane to enter while waiting for a red light to change.

For me, doubt is always present. So what is a person like me to do when it comes to choosing my spiritual path? Not making a decision is not an option, since *not* making a choice is a kind of choice by default. For instance, by 10:02 a.m., we have made the choice of whether to take the 10:00 a.m. train. And this is true for all relationships: when we *delay* choosing, we *are* choosing. When we *fail* to choose, we still *choose*.

For a few years in my spiritual journey, my habitual analysis turned into crippling paralysis. I couldn't move forward, in any direction. I felt as though I needed to get every question answered and every mystery cleared up before I took another step forward. I had already studied the teachings of the Buddha, read the Qur'an, considered a number of New Age teachers, and read all the popular pro-atheism books at the time. I eventually came to believe in Jesus stronger than ever, but I suffered under the faulty assumption that I couldn't move forward as a Christ-follower until I achieved absolute certitude in my faith.

I felt I needed to study more, reflect more, experience more, and gain more confidence before I dared identify myself to others as a follower of Jesus. Because I could second-guess anything, I suffered from imposter syndrome in everything.

This was a hard place in which to be stuck. Worst of all, I knew that Jesus' last recorded words commissioned his disciples to go and make more disciples: "Then Jesus came to them and said, 'All authority in heaven and on earth has been given to me. Therefore go and make disciples of all nations, baptizing them in the name of the Father and of the Son and of the Holy Spirit, and teaching them to obey everything I have commanded you. And surely I am with you always, to the very end of the age'" (Matthew 28:18-20).

It was one thing for me to live with my chronic doubt. It was another thing to invite other people to change their minds and their lives about that of which I myself was never fully certain.

Then one day I read the verses just before the great commission. Right before issuing those last recorded words of Jesus, Matthew describes the state of the disciples when Jesus gave these final instructions: "Then the eleven disciples went to Galilee, to the mountain where Jesus had told them to go. When they saw him, they worshiped him; but some doubted" (Matthew 28:16-17).

I had read those two verses a hundred times and never noticed what now seemed to glow on the page as though neon with supernatural highlighter. When the resurrected Jesus appeared to the disciples, "they worshiped him; but some doubted." The grammar of the original language makes it clear: all the disciples worshiped Jesus, and within that group of worshiping disciples was a subgroup of doubting-yet-worshiping disciples. You see, it is to this group of doubting worshipers that Jesus entrusted the future of his movement.

That day I realized Jesus valued me as a disciple as much as he valued anyone who never had a doubt, asked a question, or struggled with certainty. That day I realized the opposite of faith is not doubt but disbelief. *Doubt does not discredit faith.* Instead, doubt is a subcategory of faith. Thank God, a person can keep asking questions while walking with Jesus!

REASONABLE FAITH

I'm addressing these issues of doubt, worship, and belief up front because I want to talk to you about some important "F-words," starting with the most vital: *faith*. Mark Twain reflected a common misunderstanding when he wrote, "Faith is believing what you know ain't so." In other words, when you know something isn't real, but wish it was, well that's what faith is for. But this is a massive category mistake.

The biblical word for "faith" (Greek *pistis*) means to trust in a person enough to invest in that relationship. Faith isn't the absence of doubt, but it is the presence of intentional choice. Neither is faith a kind of irrational belief without evidence. Rather, faith is trust in a person based on evidence. According to the Bible, faith in God always takes our relationship beyond the evidence, but never contrary to it.

For instance, when I married Nina I had good evidence that she was a wonderful, trustworthy, and loving person. But I still didn't have conclusive evidence that she would remain all of these things for the rest of our lives together. I had observed Nina in her relationships as a sister, daughter, friend, and girlfriend, but I had never observed her as a wife or mother. That version of her didn't exist yet, so how could I *know*? People change. Circumstances change. Marriages change. And marriages change people.

But that's the point: I had enough evidence about who Nina *had been* that I could take the reasonable risk to commit to who she *would be*.

All relationship is risk. All trust is risk. All love is risk. Everything that really and truly matters is risk.

When John the Baptist was arrested and held in prison, he began to doubt (see the story in Matthew 11:1-6; Luke 7:18-23). So John sent word to Jesus asking a simple question: "Are you the Messiah or not?" Jesus' answer is illuminating. Instead of a simple "Yes, I am" or "No, I'm not," Jesus told the messengers to go back to John and report all the evidence they saw, including his many miracles, his care for the poor, and the core content of his message. In other words, Jesus invited John to arrive at his own conclusion and to trust in him *based on the evidence*. Jesus of Nazareth: the original evidentialist.

Søren Kierkegaard is known as the father of existentialism and is one of my favorite philosophers. A brilliant intellectual, he unapologetically saw belief in God as a "leap of faith," and I agree. Any meaningful relationship is. But God wants us to run the ramp of reason before we take the leap of faith.

FAITH AS RESPONSE;
OR, HOW TO RECEIVE A GIFT

When God reaches toward us with the gift of life, it's called *grace*. When we reach out and receive this gift, it's called *faith*. If grace is true, then the only thing left for us to do is *believe* it. By believing something, by trusting that it's true, we are simply receiving the gift of grace God offers. Faith is how we receive grace. What else could we do to receive a gift except trust that the gift really is a gift and that God really is that good?

When I was kid, I had a friend with a really bothersome sense of humor. He'd hold out his hand to shake mine, like some sort of little gentleman, and then when I'd reach out to take his hand, he would pull it away and say "Psych!" He thought he was really funny. Once he had a pen that I liked, and when I said so, he held it out to me and said, "Here, you take it. Really, I want you to have it. You're a good friend to me. It's yours." At first I was skeptical, but he insisted. So I smiled, said thank you, and reached out my hand to accept the gift.

You know how that story ends.

Faith means trusting that God is not playing head games with us. Faith takes God at his word and believes that God isn't going to say "Psych!" and take it all back. It means trusting God when he says he has taken care of everything and that there is nothing more we can do to achieve our salvation. God has really done it all.

The apostle Paul, aware of how "unbelievably" good the gospel is, continually hammers this reality home: "For it is by grace you have been saved, through faith—and this is not from yourselves, it is the gift of God—not by works, so that no one can boast. For we are God's handiwork, created in Christ Jesus to do good works, which God prepared in advance for us to do" (Ephesians 2:8-10). See that? Those who trust Jesus *have been* saved. It's a done deal. A given gift. No returns, no refunds, stamped it, no erasies.

We're saved not because of our good deeds, religious or humanitarian, so it's not a matter of bragging about what we have accomplished. It's true that when we trust that we have been saved by grace, we realize that we have been created to live a life of good works and loving actions. But these actions are the *result* of salvation, not the *means* to work for it. The difference is crucial. All that true believers do—live good lives, go to church, read the Bible, pray, and so on—we do for *celebration*, not for *salvation*. The pressure is off!

This is radically freeing. We are free from our guilt, our shame, and our sense of failure. We are free from the treadmill of performance-based religion. We are free from worry about what God thinks of us, and free from anxiety about our eternal destiny.

As I often tell my friends at The Meeting House: Grace means that we Christians are those peculiar people who gather together every Sunday morning to celebrate the fact that we don't *have to* gather together every Sunday morning to be saved. We read the Bible regularly to be reminded of the good news that we don't *have to* read the Bible regularly to be right with God. We sing songs of worship to express our adoration for the One who says we don't *have to* sing, or pray, or meditate, or participate in any liturgy in order to be on God's good side. Grace frees us up to celebrate God's love because we are done trying to earn it.

When we receive God's grace by faith, everything changes. That's why the gospel is called good *news* and not good *advice*. Advice is an opinion someone offers others to help them do what they should do to achieve what they want. News is an announcement about something that has already happened. Good advice says, "Here's what you need to do." Good news says, "Here's what has already been done for you."

The gospel of Jesus is good news about something already accomplished for us. This means that our response to the message of Jesus will be more along the lines of trusting and celebrating rather than working to attain something we need to accomplish. As my friend Andrew likes to say, faith just means saying "Wow" and "Thank you."

Religion offers good advice. Jesus announces good news. And it's the best news ever.

Remember when Nina proposed to me in front of our church? That was my moment of healing and wholeness in the romance department. Healing came when I opened up to the reality of just how much someone else loved me. Nina had gone to great lengths to convince me, including her daring declaration of love and commitment, and all I had to do was allow myself to accept that it was true.

God's heart is *for* us. God is bent toward us, and he has gone to extravagant lengths to demonstrate it. "But God demonstrates his own love for us in this: While we were still sinners, Christ died for us" (Romans 5:8). All we need to do is welcome in this love, to trust that it is true.

FAITH'S FLIP SIDE: REPENTANCE

In some Bible passages, repentance is listed alongside faith as our proper response to the message of God's grace. The very first sermon of Jesus recorded in Mark's gospel is simply "The time has come. . . . The kingdom of God has come near. *Repent and believe the good news!*" (Mark 1:15). Repentance is a kind of partner to faith—in fact, it's the other side of the same coin. That's why repentance is assumed whenever faith is talked about in the Bible, and vice versa (e.g., Acts 2:38; 16:30-31).

The word *repentance* comes from the Greek word *metanoia*, which means to change our way of thinking (literally, from *meta*—to change, and *noia*—to think). So Jesus is calling us all to change our old patterns of thinking and begin to trust in his good news. Repent and believe.

Turn from the weakness of romantic sentiment to the power of agape love.

Turn from the insecurity of denying your sin to the freedom of confession and forgiveness.

Turn from the addiction of self in the center to letting Jesus lead you in serving others.

Turn from the tiring treadmill of religion to the rest God gives by his grace.

Turn from life as an "I" to life as an "Us," and start your eternal, abundant life now.

It's been my prayer that you have been "repenting" the entire time you've been reading this book. I hope you have begun to see Jesus differently, to see your need in a new light, and to value God's grace as the answer to your soul's deepest longing. If so, then you're already repenting. As you take in the gospel, faith is growing.

FORGIVENESS:
ALWAYS REAL BUT NOT ALWAYS RECEIVED

When we change our way of thinking about God (repentance) and trust in his love (faith), then we are ready to receive his forgiveness, which is necessary to restore, reconcile, and reunite our broken relationship.

Forgiveness (our second F-word, if you're keeping score) happens between persons. In order for forgiveness to be fully effective, it must be offered *and* received. When that happens, broken relationships can be mended and alienated parties can be reconciled.

Yes, it is good to offer forgiveness whether or not it is ever received. Therapeutic forgiveness allows us to let go of the bitterness and judgment that is eating us up inside. So we come to the point of being willing to forgive, of filling our hearts with forgiveness for the one who has wronged us. This is good for our mental health, but so far it hasn't mended any broken relationships. Sometimes we may even need to "forgive" someone who is already dead—not for the purpose of reconciliation but for our own healing.

This illustrates how forgiveness can be real but not received. God's forgiveness for each of us is real. God's heart is filled with only forgiveness toward us for every sin we have done or will ever do. But you may not benefit from that forgiveness if you don't believe it is true. Without faith in Jesus, you may stay away from God, avoiding him, believing him to be angry with you and sickened by your sin. Much like the prodigal son before he repented.

THE PRODIGAL SON

In Luke 15, Jesus told one of his most famous stories: the parable of the prodigal son. The story shows the heart of God as our true Father and how we as his children often get it wrong in different ways. It also illustrates how grace, faith, forgiveness, and repentance all work together to reunite broken relationships.

In brief, a wealthy farmer's young adult son does an unimaginably selfish thing: he demands his father give him his share of the family inheritance early so he can go off to pursue his own ambitions. This is the equivalent to saying to his dad, "I can't wait for you to die already." Despite this cruel act of selfish entitlement (or maybe because of it), the father gives his son over to his own wishes, letting him leave with his inheritance money to live as he pleases. Eventually, after living a life of pursuing pleasure at all costs, the son runs out of money and hits rock bottom.

When the son finds himself on a farm eating pig slop as his only food (definitely an all-time low for a wealthy young Jewish man), the pain and shame of his situation becomes the incubator for *repentance*—which, remember, means *rethinking*. "I have been wrong all along," he thinks. "Maybe my father will give me a second chance, even to take a job as one of his hired hands to begin to work off my debt." This conviction of personal responsibility for wrongdoing, mixed with a ray of hope that his father's disposition toward him will not be pure hatred, pure anger, and pure punishment, is all he needs to pick himself up out of the mud and begin the journey home.

When the son arrives home, he is shocked, but not by his father's wrath, judgment, or "I told you so" lectures. He is shocked by his father's *grace*.

Jesus described the scene this way: "But while he was still a long way off, his father saw him and was filled with compassion for him; he ran to his son, threw his arms around him and kissed him" (Luke 15:20). The father doesn't just welcome his son home as a hired hand; he welcomes him home *as his son*. All is forgiven: the offense *and* the debt. What's more, the father doesn't just *accept* his son; he *celebrates* his son. He throws him a welcome home party, complete with food, music, and dancing. Now it is up to the son to show *faith* in his father's forgiveness. And when he does, they are truly reunited.

Now back it up again for a slow-motion replay. Back at the pig farm, had the prodigal son tried to console his fragile ego with lies about how he was the victim in all of this—scarred by the wounds of a harsh father, pampered by a smothering mother, abandoned by friends, misunderstood by his brother, burned by bad luck in business, and . . . and . . . and—well, he would have never taken personal responsibility for his sin, never returned home, never confessed and apologized, and never received his father's forgiveness. Likewise, had the prodigal son assumed false-hoods about his father being mad at him, awaiting him with only wrath and condemnation (which would have been justified), the son would have never returned and would have missed out on his father's love and grace.

The son didn't realize just how gracious his father really was, but he had enough faith to find out. He had enough faith to come home, to believe that life *with* his father was better than life *apart from* his father. And that was enough. It was this tiny amount of faith, the size of a mustard seed, that changed his narrative, brought him home, and put him in a position to receive all the blessings his father had ready to lavish on him.

So on the one hand, our faith doesn't make God loving or for-giving or gracious toward us. He already is all of that and more. But our *lack* of faith can keep us at a distance and prevent us from ever experiencing the reunion God wants with us.

NARROW GATE

Jesus taught that there is a "way" (sometimes translated "road" or "path") that leads to life and one that leads to death. In his famous Sermon on the Mount, Jesus said, "Enter through the narrow gate. For wide is the gate and broad is the road that leads to destruction, and many enter through it. But small is the gate and narrow the road that leads to life, and only a few find it" (Matthew 7:13-14).

A more recent treatment of this same passage reads, "There are two paths before you; you may take only one path. One doorway is narrow. And one door is wide. Go through the narrow door. For the wide door leads to a wide path, and the wide path is broad; the wide, broad path is easy, and the wide, broad, easy path has many, many people on it; but the wide, broad, easy, crowded path leads to death. Now then that narrow door leads to a narrow road that in turn leads to life. It is hard to find that road. Not many people manage it" (Matthew 7:13-14 Voice).

This book is, among other things, an invitation to choose the narrow way. (For the *Matrix* fans among us, that's the red pill.) It is not the way of the many, the mainstream, the masses. It is the way of Jesus—a way left untried by the majority, including many who have called themselves "Christians," which is something Jesus predicted (Matthew 7:21-23). G. K. Chesterton put it best: "The Christian faith has not been tried and found wanting. It has been found difficult and left untried."

When I was young, I assumed this teaching of Jesus to walk the narrow way was a challenge to keep living right, to stay on the narrow path, to keep making moral choices so that one day I could enter the narrow gate. I'd heard people talk about arriving at heaven as entering "the pearly gates," complete with Saint Peter to welcome us in, usually with some witty comment that plays well in jokes. So the long and narrow road came first, and if I stayed on it, one day I might arrive at the narrow gate.

But now I realize that I had the order completely backward, which makes all the difference in the world. The way of living good enough so that you can enter salvation at the end of your life is the way of religion. It is precisely the *opposite* of the gospel. The narrow gate that Jesus talked about in the Sermon on the Mount is not the gate of heaven. The gate he talked about is *himself*. He is the door to life. The gate comes first; *then* we walk the narrow road, in the company and friendship of Jesus.

And so we come full circle, back to the good news in one word—Jesus.

When some religious leaders challenged Jesus on his offensive message, he said, "I am the gate; whoever enters through me will be saved. They will come in and go out, and find pasture" (John 10:9). Jesus is the gate. We "enter the narrow gate" in *this* life, by faith. *Then* we begin a life of walking with Jesus—the narrow way (John 14:6)—a life of learning how to follow Jesus with gratitude for the salvation we have already received.

Yes, this way is narrow, and only a few people find it. To be a Christ-follower is to embrace the way of the minority. It is also a way of joy, freedom, and a generosity of spirit, born out of gratitude for God's grace to us. And it can also be a way of hardship because of the misunderstandings and even persecution of others. Jesus warns his followers to be ready for a response from others that is, well, less than supportive (see John 15:18-21).

COUNT THE COST

It's time to have a hard talk.

The first F-word (*faith*) opens us up to receive another F-word (*forgiveness*), which prepares us for a life of the third F-word: *following*.

The apostle James wrote, "Faith by itself, if it is not accompanied by action, is dead" (James 2:17). Faith is trust, and if we trust Jesus, we will listen to him when he says, "Follow me." Someone who responds to Jesus by saying "Oh, I trust you Jesus, completely. I just don't want to follow you" probably doesn't really trust him in the first place. We have a word for people who say they believe something but don't act on it: *hypocrite*. Neither Jesus nor you wants you to be that.

Suppose you were lost in the woods and you met a man who said, "I know the way out. Trust me. Let's go this way. Follow me." If you really did *trust* him, how would you show it? Easy peasy: you would *follow* him. And if you didn't follow him, that would be a sign that you didn't trust him. This is how it is with faith and following Jesus.

Now, if you think you might be ready to follow Jesus, then Jesus has one more thing to say to you before you take your next step. Sometimes people would run up to Jesus with enthusiasm and declare their loyalty. They were excited by his irreligious message, but maybe for the wrong reasons. Perhaps they just loved seeing Jesus "stick it to the man of organized religion." Perhaps they were attracted to the anti-institutional side of Jesus' teaching. But Jesus never wanted followers to build their lives on being anti-anything. Jesus wanted his followers to be pro-something—or better, pro-Some*one*.

So when Jesus sensed that somebody was coming to him with the right enthusiasm but the wrong motivation, he would throw down a hard truth. To a rich man, he said to sell everything and give it to the poor. To a man who loved his family more than anything, Jesus said to leave his family and come follow him. And to a man who loved comfort and was attracted to Jesus for all the blessings he would receive by following him, Jesus said, "Foxes have dens and birds have nests, but the Son of Man has no place to lay his head" (Matthew 8:20). In other words, "Even the animals have a place to sleep tonight, but not me. Are you sure you want to join my movement?"

In order to do justice to the call of Christ, I want to give you that same opportunity to first count the cost. The salvation that Jesus offers is a free gift of grace—but it can cost you everything. Yes, God has paid the price, and all we have to do is accept this by faith. There is nothing we can do to earn what is given as a gift. But that gift is life, and that life starts now, and we live that wonderful, Jesus-shaped life by laying down our lives in the love of others, including our enemies, just as Jesus did.

The most attractive, kindhearted, and seemingly unattainable person in the world could tell you, "I want to marry you," and that would be an amazing gift of grace. But if that person really meant it, and you really got married, you would still have to live with that person, and that always takes work. So you need to count the cost—not just the cost of a wedding, but also the lifetime cost of the energy, attention, and investment involved in a marriage.

This is why Jesus said, "Whoever wants to be my disciple must deny themselves and take up their cross and follow me" (Mark 8:34). Some sales pitch, Jesus! But in the next verse he continued, "For whoever wants to save their life will lose it, but whoever loses their life for me and for the gospel will find it." Jesus is showing us the only way to truly live—the way of letting our ego die and allowing the love life God describes in the gospel to become our everything.

On another occasion, when large crowds were following Jesus, thinking he was offering them an easy pathway to prosperity, he said, "Suppose one of you wants to build a tower. Won't you first sit down and estimate the cost to see if you have enough money to complete it? For if you lay the foundation and are not able to finish it, everyone who sees it will ridicule you, saying, 'This person began to build and wasn't able to finish'" (Luke 14:28-30). There is something worse than never trusting Jesus: trusting him for a while and then turning back (Luke 9:62). There is something worse than staying single: getting married and then going through the pain of divorce.

Our lives are like building projects. The first step is to choose the right foundation. Jesus said, "Therefore everyone who hears these words of mine and puts them into practice is like a wise man who built his house on the rock" (Matthew 7:24). Notice that the wise builder didn't *just* choose the solid foundation of Jesus and his teachings; he actually built something. That's what we do when we apply what we learn. We reject the temptation toward hypocrisy (learning lots but applying little), and we allow the teachings and example of Jesus to help us shape our lives.

But before all of that, Jesus says, a wise builder counts the cost. A wise builder doesn't run headlong into a building project without enough financing, lest he or she get halfway done and cannot complete the project. Jesus says when people are eager to make the right decision for the wrong reason—eager to follow him because they want a life that's easy instead of a life of love (which is never easy)—they might abandon the Christ life halfway, and that is worse than if they had never said yes to Jesus in the first place. Now their on-again, off-again lives with Jesus are standing as a monument to failure. God's grace never fails, but our best intentions often do.

So Jesus simply invites every eager would-be follower to count the cost first. Are you willing to give your whole life to Jesus?

READY TO SETTLE DOWN?

The life of *faith* in Jesus that opens us up to receiving the *forgiveness* of God and prepares us for *following* Jesus as our Lord leads to the last F-word: *friendship*. God wants to be not just your good friend but your best friend, your life partner, your spiritual husband.

Some people prefer to keep their options open. They "play the field" with a variety of worldviews and refuse to settle down while life passes them by. I get it. I was there once. But had I stayed in that limbo for long, I would have missed out on so much.

Because of our fear of commitment, many of us sample from Jesus, enjoying a taste of his teaching when we like it, before moving on to sample the next attractive spiritual sound bite we come across. That's smorgasbord spirituality.

Maybe you've been spiritually hurt before. Perhaps you've been bruised by organized religion in general or religious people in particular. If so, I understand your temptation to remain untethered, drawing bits and pieces from all religions and philosophies, like some sort of belief buffet. Some people can go their whole lives borrowing from all but committing to none. They are like people addicted to the romance of dating but afraid of the hard work of marriage—always up for new adventures but never willing to "settle down." For a while this seems thrilling. But as life moves on, we mature and realize that we have missed out on some of the beauty of being human—growing old together, with the love only relational consistency can create.

I've met people like this, who often say things like "I'm a person of faith" or "I'm into faith" or "I have a strong faith," but never talk about what or who their faith is *in*. That's the wrong use of the F-word.

These people are flirting with faith but never actually trusting. Remember, faith is a *connecting* word—faith is what connects persons. It means I have complete trust in someone or something. Faith means I have chosen to rely on a *particular* person or perspective to guide my life. Faith, then, is only as valuable and as powerful as the person or perspective we place it in.

Once we know Jesus, identifying as a "person of faith" is like someone who has met their soul mate describing themselves as "a person of love" or "a person of marriage." But people in love don't talk about love as a detached topic—they talk about *the person* they love. They don't say they want "marriage" as a thing—they say they want to marry *the person* they love.

So I am not inviting you to become "a person of faith." How boring! How relationally vapid! How spiritually hollow! I am inviting you to fall in love with *Jesus*, to trust in *Jesus*, and to choose to commit your whole life to *Jesus*.

It's time to ask whether fear is holding you back from genuine faith. This book is my invitation to you to commit. It's my proposal that you say "I do" to the joyful experience of discovering the life you were made to live: a life embraced by and committed to Jesus. Are you ready to tie the knot?

EPILOGUE
NOW WHAT?

I had been my whole life a bell, and never knew
it until at that moment I was lifted and struck.
—ANNIE DILLARD

I have a question for you. Which are you? You've finished reading through a book entitled *Reunion: The Good News of Jesus for Seekers, Saints, and Sinners.* So which are you?

Let's review in reverse order.

SINNER?

Are you a sinner? Absolutely (not).

On the one hand, we are all sinners, "for all have sinned and fall short of the glory of God" (Romans 3:23). The apostle Paul wrote, "Christ Jesus came into the world to save sinners—of whom I am the worst" (1 Timothy 1:15). Even after receiving the forgiving acceptance of Jesus, Paul saw himself as a sinner, present tense. (Paul had been involved in the persecution of Christians before he became one, so that explains the "worst" bit.)

But Paul also saw himself as forgiven, cleansed, and reunited, which means that being a sinner was no longer his primary identity. On one occasion, when lamenting that he still sometimes gave in to temptation, Paul made this adjustment to his self-understanding: "Now if I do what I do not want to do, *it is no longer I who do it, but it is sin living in me that does it"* (Romans 7:20). If I follow this line of reasoning, then when I sin, these sinful thoughts or actions are not what I (the true "I") really want. They are old habits and peripheral aspects of my persona. But the true me no longer wants sin. The true me has tasted the goodness of God's grace and wants more and more of God. For a forgiven, cleansed, and reconciled Christ-follower (should you choose to accept this mission), sin is still possible, and may even be pleasurable in fleeting ways, but it will never fully satisfy, because it isn't part of who we really are.

Have you ever seen those pictures of someone with an angel on one shoulder and a devil on the other? It represents the universal human experience of having two opposite and dueling forces inside us. Our id and our superego, in Freudian terms, vie for the attention of our ego. When we are in the middle of those times of competing inner impulses, we can feel fractured, split down the middle, half bad and half good. But Jesus assures us that for Christ-followers, the struggle to make consistently loving choices is a battle not between equal but opposite internal forces (e.g., your good half and your evil half), but between your real self and your false self, your spirit and your flesh, your inner person and your peripheral persona, your center and your circumference.

This doesn't mean that we start to live perfect, spiritually mature lives free from all failure. But it does mean that our spirit—the heart of who we are—is remade, cleansed, and empowered here and now. And that will make a difference in how we see ourselves, and in how we approach all our relationships and all our choices.

SAINT?

Are you a saint? The choice is yours. If you have received God's grace by faith, then you *are* a saint.

I know we think of saints as special super-Christians in medieval iconography, often depicted with the warm glow of a golden halo. But the word *saint* means "holy one," and this is the beautiful message of the gospel: holiness, or righteousness, is not a spiritual state for us to achieve through our exemplary lives but is a freely given gift from God that we simply receive by faith.

If you are reunited with God through Christ, then you are holy. You are a saint.

When people in the early church wrote letters to each other, they addressed all the believers as "saints" (see, e.g., Romans 1:7; 1 Corinthians 1:2; Colossians 1:2). To be holy simply means to be set apart for a special purpose, and that is definitely true for all those who follow Jesus. There was never a special class of super-Christian called "saints" in the early church. No Christian, whether alive or dead, was venerated as somehow more special than the rest of the family of faith. Rather, everyone considered themselves and all other Christians to be saints of God.

So next time you struggle with temptation, or find yourself fighting against sinful desires, remember who you *really* are and what you *really* want. You may still be a sinner in some capacity, but you are far more of a saint than sinner. Your status as "sinner" is a lingering part of your past, but your status as "saint" is a very present part of your future.

Take this advice from the apostle Paul: "This one thing I do: *forgetting what lies behind and straining forward to what lies ahead, I press on* toward the goal for the prize of the heavenly call of God in Christ Jesus" (Philippians 3:13-14 NRSV). The Greek words behind "straining forward" and "I press on" in the original manuscripts mean to stretch out to grasp, and to chase after, to pursue, even to hunt down. Our focus as Christ-followers is not on who we *were* (we forget that) but who we *are becoming*. We chase after and hunt down our true identity every day, in every moment, with every choice and every new decision we make.

As a saint, you are no longer a product of your past, but a product of your future. The only thing about your past that defines you is the life, death, and life again of Jesus Christ. May you live every moment of every day with a renewed attitude and a clarified vision of who you really are and are becoming.

Welcome to sainthood!

SEEKER?

Are you a seeker? I hope so. Don't ever stop. A Christ-follower has already found ultimate purpose and meaning in the God-who-is-love, but still seeks to experience that love more and more.

Jesus said, "Ask and it will be given to you; seek and you will find; knock and the door will be opened to you. For everyone who asks receives; the one who seeks finds; and to the one who knocks, the door will be opened" (Luke 11:9-10). He then went on to say that the focus of our asking, knocking, and seeking should be more of God, the presence of his Holy Spirit.

The apostle Paul told people who were already Christians, saints of God, to "be filled with the Spirit" (Ephesians 5:18). We are all responsible for seeking out more of God and for letting our lives be filled up with his presence. Don't assume you already have all the God you are ever going to get; rather, continually seek out a deeper experience of his Spirit.

This is not a pressure-filled search with dire consequences if we fail. This is more like an already loved spouse desiring more and more intimacy with the one who already loves him or her. We don't want to waste a day not growing closer.

How do we do this? How do we seek after more and more of God's Spirit? How can we take responsibility for the command to "be filled with the Spirit"? While this is the topic for another book, for now I can say this much. Think of your life like a home and God as your heavenly spouse. You got married and moved into your home together as true life partners. But after the wedding, instead of doing all of life together, you relocated God down into the basement of your subconscious. Now he is more like a tenant who rents a room downstairs than he is your daily partner in all things. You might check in on him once a week or so, to make sure he's still there and you're still on good terms, but then you go back to your daily life in functional bachelor/bachelorette mode. You are vaguely aware that God is around somewhere, and if someone asked you, you might genuinely say, "Yes, I love God very much.

We do all of life together." But practically speaking, God is more like your tenant than your spouse.

Every important love relationship deserves daily investment. To be "filled with the Spirit" is to invite God out of the basement of our subconscious and into the day-by-day, moment-by-moment awareness that we are doing life together, that God is with us in every decision and experience, and that we are being loved and being invited to love in every moment. To be filled with the Spirit is to consciously *be* with God, to invite God to lead you, to talk with God and to listen to God, and to love other people with the love of God, consciously aware and enjoying that you are doing all things *together*.

SAYING "I DO"

Let me share four core convictions that have motivated me to write this book and that I believe have motivated you to read it.

First, the apostle John claimed that just by entering human history, Jesus brought light to all people (John 1:4-5, 9). Jesus is helping you see everything more clearly.

Second, Jesus himself claimed that through his death on the cross, he would personally draw all of us to himself (John 12:32). You are being pulled toward Jesus.

Third, Jesus also said the Spirit of God would convict everyone of what is wrong and pull us all toward what is right (John 16:8-11). To the extent you are listening to the gentle whisper of God's Spirit, you are becoming aware of what you need to leave behind as well as what you really want to embrace.

Fourth, whenever we pay attention to the good news of Jesus, our faith grows (Romans 10:17). The gospel comes with its own power pack. The message itself generates the faith it takes to believe it and receive it. You are ready to respond.

The apostle John was up front about why he wrote his biography of Jesus. "These are written that you may believe that Jesus is the Messiah, the Son of God, and that by believing you may have life in his name" (John 20:31). That's it.

That's why I wrote this book, too. I wrote this book about (re)union so that you may believe that Jesus is the Messiah (the one who delivers us from our sin and separation from God) and the Son of God (the one who truly shows us who God is and who we were meant to be), and that by believing in Jesus, you might have life in his name (that is, the full life God has always intended for you).

So are you ready now to say "I do" to Jesus' proposal? If so, I'd love to assist you in saying your vows.

The last chapter of the Bible includes an invitation to receive the free gift of God's grace. The invitation is given by the Spirit of God himself *and* by the bride of Christ, the church. "The Spirit and the bride say, 'Come!' And let the one who hears say, 'Come!' Let the one who is thirsty come; and let the one who wishes take the free gift of the water of life" (Revelation 22:17).

Followers of Jesus, like me, get to invite others to accept God's grace. So I'm ending this book by inviting you to come home to God and accept his embrace. If your soul is thirsty for more, then I hope you respond to this invitation. If you feel you're ready to receive this gift and come alive to the love and life Jesus has for you, then here are some simple things you can do right now.

For starters, you could take some time to pray. We've been talking a lot *about* God in this book. If you haven't started already, now could be your time to begin to talk *to* God.

If praying on your own feels too intimidating for you, then I'm happy to suggest a prayer or two that you could make your own.

Below is a prayer you can pray. It gives you an opportunity to begin to express your love, your faith, and your gratitude to God for the gospel. There is nothing magical about these words. They are an opportunity to express your heart. You can read them verbatim or express these thoughts to God in your own words. Some couples like to repeat their wedding vows after the minister word for word, and others like to write their own. Either way, it's the heart that counts.

Read this prayer over, think about it, and if it captures where your heart is in this moment, then make these words your words and this prayer your prayer.

Dear God,

Thank you for this good news about your love for me and the life you have for me. I accept your gift of salvation, and I trust in Jesus to be my Lord, my Leader, my Master, and my Mentor. I'm sorry for my sins, and I thank you for your forgiveness. I no longer want to run away from you, or ignore you, or live for any purpose other than you. Thank you for being my friend. I'm excited to be yours.

Amen.

If this prayer represents your heart, then I want to be among the first to say, "Welcome to the family!" Through Jesus, we are brothers and sisters. You are a part of something that's off the map. It stretches around the world and backward and forward through time—the family of faith, the body of Christ, the bride of Jesus, the gathering of God's people. The church.

But maybe you're not there yet. Maybe you're still undecided or feeling firmly noncommittal. All right, let's work with that.

Maybe you feel you need more time before making a commitment. Believe me, I get you. Maybe you need to step away and think, research, discuss, ponder, and pray. My only suggestion would be that you keep on asking, seeking, and knocking on heaven's door. God has brought you this far, and he's not giving up, so please don't either.

Maybe you can't yet say that you want to follow Jesus, but maybe you *want* to want to follow Jesus. You've made it this far in the book, invested this much time and thought, which suggests to me that you're taking this seriously. Perhaps you are feeling the pull of God or sensing the ring of truth in the message of Jesus.

One time a man with a small amount of faith said to Jesus, "I do believe; help me overcome my unbelief!" (Mark 9:24). Does that describe you? Do you have just enough faith to ask God to help you overcome your lack of faith? You might want to pray something like this:

Dear God,

I don't know what I believe. But here I am, talking to you, willing to learn, and wanting to grow. I think there might be something to this whole Jesus thing, and I'm asking you to please confirm the truth of his message to my heart. If I'm going to follow Jesus, I know I'll need help, from you and from others. I'm ready to receive whatever help you choose to give me.

Thank you.

Amen.

NOW WHAT?

Now what? Here are some possible next steps. This isn't a "to do" list as much as a "to be" list. Turning our faith into action is how we become our true selves.

1. *Tell somebody.* The gospel is a relational message, and it will feel incomplete inside us when we keep it to ourselves rather than express it within relationships. You can start by letting me know. Get in touch with me, Bruxy Cavey: weird name, which should make me easy to find on social media. I'd love to celebrate with you! And if someone gave you this book, close the loop with that person. I'll bet she or he would love to talk with you about it.

2. *Go to church.* Start looking for a good church. You were designed to grow spiritually in the context of intimate and interactive relationships with people walking along the same path. Talk to a pastor or leaders at the church you attend or are considering attending. Tell them about this book and your follow-up questions. If a church leader isn't eager to talk about your questions, you're at the wrong church.

3. *Share this book.* You may already be thinking of people you know who are looking for the freedom and the fresh

start that only Jesus offers. Don't keep it to yourself. And at the same time, don't be discouraged if their reaction isn't the same as yours. This message is universal, but faith is personal.

4. *Start a group.* When you do find people with a shared interest in learning more about Jesus, you might want to start a discussion group or a book club. A different kind of learning happens when we engage in conversation, hear how other people are processing, and have to work at finding the words to express our own journey.

5. *Read it again.* Whether as part of a group or on your own, the message of this book is a message that bears repeating. We can never get enough of the gospel inside us. The gospel is more than the message that leads us to Jesus; it is the message that Jesus uses to lead us with. So read this book again, *slowly.* Get a Bible and start looking up the Scripture references, reading them in context and making notes. Check out the supplemental materials available in print and online. Before you begin each session, pray and ask God to teach you. Before you end each session, pray and thank God for what he has done for you and is doing in you.

6. *Get baptized.* Ya, you heard me. Baptism is a beautiful symbol of our salvation that God can use to remind us of the gospel for the rest of our lives. God made us physical beings, and he offers us physical ways to remind ourselves of spiritual truths. Through baptism, we physically declare to ourselves and others what we know to be spiritually true: we have died to our old life, been cleansed from all our sin, and raised again to new life in Christ. If you are ready to say yes to following Jesus, express it through baptism.

7. *Talk daily.* The most intimate relationships thrive through daily interaction. Jesus expected God's children to want to talk to their heavenly Father every day (Matthew 6:11),

since he is talking with us all the time. Get a Bible and start with the Gospels. Set a few minutes aside every day to read a bit (that's you listening to God), and then pray about what you've read (that's you talking with God), and then meditate on whatever God has highlighted to your mind (that's you letting it all sink in). Reading gets the information into your mind; meditation is like hitting the enter key for your heart. Set time aside to relate to God this way every day, and watch how your mind, your heart, your life changes.

8. *Cultivate awareness.* Once you are committed to spending time every day focusing on and learning more about your love life with God, you can move forward to inviting God into every moment. The apostle Paul said that God wants us to "pray continually" (1 Thessalonians 5:16-18). This refers to a kind of unceasing, ongoing, moment-by-moment awareness that we are not doing life alone, that we are with our greatest love, and that we refuse to ignore God's presence, even when involved in the many activities of our lives. All of life is better when you live it with your best friend.

9. *Serve Jesus through others.* One of the ways we can be close to Jesus is by serving the needs of others. When we serve the poor and marginalized the way Jesus did, Jesus takes it personally. "Truly I tell you," he will say on judgment day, "whatever you did for one of the least of these brothers and sisters of mine, you did for me" (see Matthew 25:31-46). And when we hurt other people, Jesus takes that personally too (Acts 9:4-5). When we love God, we will love the people he loves (1 John 4:12, 20), and when we love those people, we are drawing closer to Jesus.

10. *Put on the new you.* Every decision you make is an opportunity to become more of who you really are—or to thoughtlessly obey the parasitic impulses that belong in your past. When talking about saying no to things that

grieve the Holy Spirit in you, such as anger, slander, greed, and lack of forgiveness, the apostle Paul wrote, "You were taught, with regard to your former way of life, to put off your old self, which is being corrupted by its deceitful desires; to be made new in the attitude of your minds; and to put on the new self, created to be like God in true righteousness and holiness" (Ephesians 4:22-24). Make every choice consciously, because every choice is spiritually powerful.

WHO ARE YOU?

You are a kite, created by God, attached by faith, guided by Christ, lifted high with the wind of the Spirit.

You are a prodigal son or daughter, returning home to find your father already looking for you and eager to throw a party.

You are the bride of Christ, desired and pursued by him and now ready to begin your love life together.

Take a moment, breathe, and let it all sink in.

The apostle Paul wrote a prayer for the first-century Christians that is recorded in Ephesians 3:14-19. He wanted everyone to move beyond believing in Jesus to really experiencing the fullness of God's love for them. And this is my prayer for all of us.

For this reason I kneel before the Father, from whom every family in heaven and on earth derives its name. I pray that out of his glorious riches he may strengthen you with power through his Spirit in your inner being, so that Christ may dwell in your hearts through faith. And I pray that you, being rooted and established in love, may have power, together with all the Lord's holy people, to grasp how wide and long and high and deep is the love of Christ, and to know this love that surpasses knowledge—that you may be filled to the measure of all the fullness of God.

Amen.

ACKNOWLEDGMENTS

I am very grateful for the help of some special people on this project.

Nina, my wife, continues to be my best friend, encourager, critic, and partner. "Thou art as wise as thou art beautiful."

My uncle Stu was my pastor during my formative young adult years, and all those years' worth of sermons built into me an ongoing love of learning and joy in Jesus.

Andrew Farley inspires me to always grow in my appreciation of the grace, love, and life of God. This book grew out of a joint project with Andrew, and I'm grateful for the ways he has helped and continues to help shape my thinking.

Nabeel Qureshi, my friend and hero in the faith, has encouraged me in speaking out about the peaceable, nonviolent nature of Christ's kingdom and has helped me see the extent to which the gospel is packed into the word *Immanuel* (God with us).

Rick Maranta has helped edit and craft this manuscript in significant ways. His fingerprints can be found throughout. (Wash your hands better, Rick.)

Valerie Weaver-Zercher has been my primary editor at Herald Press; Amy Gingerich has overseen this project; Melodie Davis has managed multiple rounds of corrections; and Dorothy Hartman has kept track of innumerable details. All are a delight to work with. Sara Versluis is the copyeditor, and Im amaze at how meny mistake she catch in thes manuscript.

Joe Questel, LeAnn Hamby, and the whole marketing team at Herald Press are doing a bang-up job at book promotion. Now stop reading this and get to work.

Greg Best, Keturah Knapp, Rebecca Thomson, and Anita Giardina have also invested significant amounts of time in this project and provided important feedback along the way. I'm blessed with wonderful friends!

Debby Barrette is a long-time friend who hasn't helped me at all on this writing project.

Okay. Debby didn't help me on *this* project, but she did help a lot on my last book, *The End of Religion*, and I forgot to thank her in the acknowledgments then, so this is my big chance. Thank you, Dee!

Matt Vincent, a dear friend and partner in ministry, leads a wonderful church-planting network also called Reunion, and has kindly navigated with me the awkwardness of me using the same name for this book. Thank you, Matt, for your grace and ongoing partnership.

Rod Tombs and Darrell Winger serve alongside me in giving leadership to The Meeting House family of churches. These two gentle giants (spiritually speaking), along with an amazing team of staff and volunteers, help all of us at The Meeting House live out the gospel rather than just talk about it.

Which brings me to all of my church family at The Meeting House. What a privilege to do life together with you special people. We live the Jesus life imperfectly, but we live it *together*. And I can't think of any other way I would want to spend another day in this world.

THE AUTHOR

Bruxy Cavey is the author of the bestselling book *The End of Religion* and senior pastor at The Meeting House, a church for people who aren't into church. The Meeting House is a multisite Anabaptist congregation in Ontario, Canada, where thousands of people connect with God and each other through Sunday services, online interaction, and a widespread house church network.

Bruxy and his wife, Nina, have three daughters and live in Hamilton, Ontario.

Connect with Bruxy at Bruxy.com or on social media. You can learn more about The Meeting House and listen to Bruxy's teaching at TheMeetingHouse.com.

a STUDY GUIDE
for SEEKERS, SAINTS, *and* SINNERS

YOU'VE READ IT. NOW TALK ABOUT IT.

The message of Jesus changed the world . . . until the world changed the message. Designed to be used with *Reunion* by Bruxy Cavey, this eight-session study guide will help you and your group learn, commit to, and share the real message of Jesus Christ with others. **2018. 96 pages. PB. 9781513802527. $9.99 USD**

Key Features
- Thought-provoking discussion questions for groups
- Prayer prompts and journaling space
- Scripture passages for inspiration and reflection
- Links to online videos and resources